Israel:
Crossroads of Conflict

Removing rock from a Roman bath at Masada

Israel :
Crossroads
of Conflict

by **Lawrence H. Feigenbaum**
and **Kalman Seigel**

ILLUSTRATED WITH PHOTOGRAPHS AND MAPS

 RAND M^CNALLY & COMPANY

Contents

30208

Picture Credits

THE AUTHORS are grateful for permission to reproduce the photographs in this book. All pictures not specifically indicated below were supplied by Israel Information Services, New York. The pictures on pages 17, 22, 30, 82, 83, and 115 (top) are from the Photographic Archives of the Jewish Theological Seminary of America, New York (Frank J. Darmstaedter); those on pages 32 and 36 are from the Zionist Archives and Library of the Palestine Foundation Fund; those on pages 63, 70, and 130 are from the Information Department of the Jewish Agency and the World Zionist Organization of Jerusalem; those on page 145 are from the Israel Trade Commission.

The maps were drawn by Don Pitcher from maps originally prepared by the Survey of Israel and Carta, Jerusalem.

Illustrations

1 The Meaning of Israel Today

For thousands of years, Israel has had a special meaning for people all over the world. As the land of the Bible, its towns and streams and mountains provide the background for the greatest stories ever told. As the Holy Land of three world religions, its history is woven into the heritage and faith of millions of people.

But the Israel of today is no mere museum piece, no quaint national park where, bypassed by the currents of modern life, antiquity has remained carefully preserved. Instead, Israel is a vital young nation, reborn almost miraculously in fulfillment of an age-old promise, certain to figure in the great events of the future.

As the homeland of a determined people with a continuous tradition of thousands of years, Israel has a meaning at a time when "alienation" and "the search for identity" are the clichés of the day. As a nation recently emerged from colonialism, it has a meaning for the scores of new Asiatic and African countries struggling with the problems of statehood.

A successful example of political independence combined with democratic institutions and technological progress, Israel is an

9

inspiration and mentor to the infant nations just freed from imperialism. Its development into a modern industrial state despite limited natural resources, hostile neighbors, and population problems constitutes a pilot demonstration project for such countries as Senegal, Liberia, Kenya, Nepal, Nigeria, and Uganda.

In area, Israel—according to its prewar 1967 boundaries—is no larger than the state of New Jersey. The entire length of the country can be spanned in a single day's driving, and its greatest width, at Beersheba, is only seventy miles. The narrow waist of Israel, along the shore of the Mediterranean Sea just above Tel Aviv, is ten miles wide, while the southernmost strip on the Gulf of Aqaba (shown on Israeli maps as the Gulf of Eilat) extends just six miles from the Egyptian to the Jordanian border. By American standards, Israel is indeed a pygmy among nations.

The size of Israel obviously cannot explain its geographical importance. But a world map or globe shows why it has been coveted by conquerors since ancient times. A bridge between East and West, it stands astride the major trade routes. From a military point of view, it commands a strategic position, fronting on the Mediterranean and overlooking the vital Sinai peninsula and the Red Sea.

The nation's population—just over two and a half million—is not as large as that of Chicago, Los Angeles, or even Brooklyn, New York. A demographic survey of the country reveals that most Israelis were not born there; in one of the most remarkable folk migrations in history, more than a million of them have come since 1948 from seventy different countries and from every continent. They include people of every race, speaking dozens of different languages. Many are the dispossessed survivors of Nazi Germany's

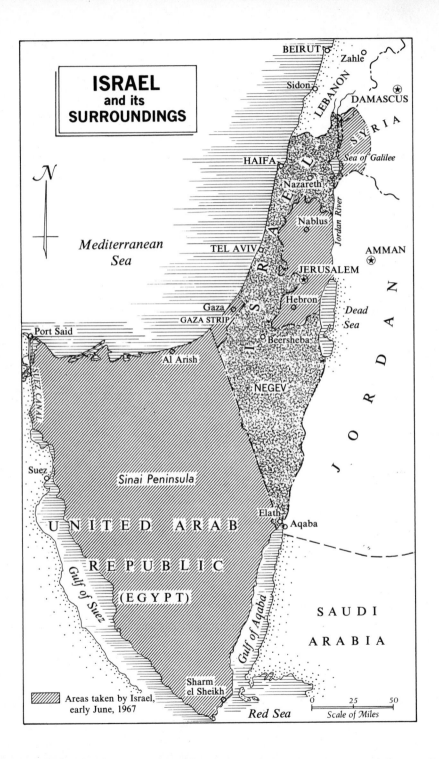

ISRAEL
and its
SURROUNDINGS

*Mediterranean
Sea*

BEIRUT
Zahle
Sidon
LEBANON
DAMASCUS
SYRIA
HAIFA
Sea of Galilee
Nazareth
Jordan River
Nablus
ISRAEL
TEL AVIV
AMMAN
JERUSALEM
Hebron
Gaza
GAZA STRIP
*Dead
Sea*
Port Said
Beersheba
Al Arish
NEGEV
JORDAN
Suez
Sinai Peninsula
SUEZ CANAL
Elath
Aqaba
U N I T E D   A R A B
R E P U B L I C
(E G Y P T)
Gulf of Suez
Gulf of Aqaba
S A U D I

A R A B I A
Sharm
el Sheikh
Red Sea

Areas taken by Israel,
early June, 1967

0   25   50
Scale of Miles

concentration camps, seeking to build new lives in their ancestral homeland.

The government has proclaimed Israel a Jewish state, and the large majority of its inhabitants are of the Jewish religion. Yet among the population, practicing their faiths freely, are hundreds of thousands of Arab Moslems and tens of thousands of Christians, including members of the Roman Catholic, Greek Orthodox, Lutheran, Baptist, and Presbyterian churches.

The Jewish community itself is divided into Ashkenazi and Sephardic branches, and into smaller sects such as the Karaites and the Samaritans. In religious practice, there is a broad spectrum, ranging from the extreme orthodox to the completely non-observant.

The language of Israel is Hebrew, the language of the Bible, revived in living speech after nearly two thousand years as a so-called "dead" language. Today, people in Israel discuss atomic energy and space travel in the same vocabulary and accents as those used by David in his Psalms and Isaiah in his prophecies.

The history of Israel is a magnificent epic. It is also the stuff of legend and folklore, richly laced with poetic symbolism and wisdom. And, as it comes down to today, it is the story of how a nation—to whom "peace" (*shalom*) is both a greeting and a farewell, as well as an article of faith—found itself locked once again in a grim battle for survival.

Israel has a particular meaning for Americans: a land of immigrants who fled from persecution . . . pioneers along an unfriendly frontier, with plow and gun at hand . . . a nation bold and confident in the face of dangers from within and without . . . How familiar it all seems!

Moslems worshipping in a famous mosque in Acre

2 In the Beginning

T he history of Israel spans almost all of recorded time. Its beginnings date back four thousand years and overlap the rise and fall of such storied civilizations as the Egyptian, the Phoenician, the Assyrian, and the Babylonian. Later, Israel runs a parallel course on the time line of history with the mighty empires of ancient Greece and Rome.

Through its first ten centuries, Israel, as might be expected, experienced good times and bad, periods of dominance and subjection. As in the history of all nations, there were battles and heroes and kings. Indeed, it might be open to question whether any purpose is served by tracing the course of events from such remote beginnings.

But the people of Israel today are strongly motivated by a sense of their history. Through the ages, it has been the bedrock of their faith, a source of inspiration, and at times a burden. No other modern nation has such continuity with the distant past; nor does antiquity seem so recent anywhere else in the world. In fact, the state of Israel would never have been founded if the Jewish people had not based their claim on ancestral memories bridging a hundred generations. It is impossible, therefore, to understand the spirit of the land without some knowledge of the main outlines of its historical development.

At the outset, some terms that are often interchangeably and imprecisely used should be defined. First of all, some distinction must be made between "Israeli" and "Jew": a citizen of Israel is not necessarily Jewish, and most Jews are not Israelis. Nevertheless, the history of Israel is, at least up to the present time, the story of the Jewish people.

The land has been called by different names over the centuries: Canaan, Judah, Judea, Palestine, Zion, Israel—each has referred at different times to a country occupying the same general geographical area, a narrow strip extending "from Dan to Beersheba" and beyond to Eilat.

Under any name, for thousands of years Jews throughout the world have regarded this small section of the earth's surface as the land of their fathers. It has figured prominently in their prayers and traditions. "If I forget thee, O Jerusalem, may my right hand forget its cunning," sang the Psalmist. "Next year in Jerusalem" is still the hope expressed all over the world as part of the Passover ritual.

Always useful citizens of the countries in which they lived, many Jews have nevertheless looked toward Israel as their literal Promised Land. On the other hand, others have viewed Israel as purely a spiritual home, a sentiment shared with Christians and Mohammedans.

The opening chapters of the history of Israel, as well as the history of the Jews, are contained in that library of books collectively known as the Bible. The Bible has long been revered as a book of devotion; in more recent times, it has been appreciated as the greatest work of world literature. But scholars in the past were inclined to discount its value as history, pointing to apparently contradictory passages and implausible episodes. Modern research and the discoveries of archeology and anthropology, however, have confirmed the essential historicity of the Bible.

The Biblical account tells of the migration of the first "Ibrim" or Hebrews—translated as "men from beyond the Euphrates"— into Canaan at about 1800 b.c. According to the book of Genesis, among these migrants was Abraham, who had turned from the polytheism (worship of many gods) practiced in his native Mesopotamia to a belief in one God. A divine promise was given to Abraham upon his arrival in Canaan: "To thy seed will I give this land."

The ancient chronicle traces the generations of Abraham through Isaac, his son, and Jacob, his grandson. With the twelve sons of Jacob, the descendants of Abraham became a fairly numerous clan.

Jacob was later honored by the name "Israel," and his sons were widely known as the children of Israel. The name was applied in turn to their descendants as a distinct people. Only about a thousand years later did the term "Jew" come into widespread use as a synonym.

But the clan of Abraham did not remain in Canaan for long. The Bible relates the story of the sons of Jacob—Joseph and his brethren—and tells how Joseph, at first sold into slavery and taken to Egypt, came to be a favorite of the ruling Pharaoh. Occupying a position of high importance in Egypt, he had his father and brothers join him in the capital of the ancient empire which, at the time, held most of the neighboring nations within its sphere of influence.

Slaves doing brickwork, about 1450 B.C.

Under the Egyptian dynasty of the Hyksos, the people of Israel enjoyed considerable prosperity. But in time, other Pharaohs came to power "who knew not Joseph." In the tangled history of the period, through dynastic, religious, imperialistic, and civil wars, the position of the Israelites in Egypt grew worse. They were enslaved and forced to build the fortresses and monuments which, magnificent even in ruin, still stand today. In their misery, the people of Israel thought again of the land promised to the descendants of Abraham which they had left centuries earlier.

A national and religious leader arose—Moses, who was raised as an Egyptian prince and educated at the royal court. Aroused by the sufferings of the Israelites and inspired by divine revelation, Moses determined to lead his people back toward Canaan and

Passover Seder in a Tel Aviv home

freedom. This mass migration—the Biblical "exodus" from Egypt
and slavery—took place in about 1220 B.C., an event celebrated in
the traditional Feast of Passover.

A generation passed as the people of Israel made their way
to the Promised Land. Many memorable incidents are recorded:
the waters of an arm of the Red Sea ebbed long enough to assure
safe passage to the refugees; the Ten Commandments and the

Torah (a way of life or law to guide the people) were revealed; stirring military victories, such as the battle of Jericho, were won over hostile tribesmen who tried to bar the way back to Canaan. In the course of the journey, Moses died, and other leaders, notably Joshua, continued the long trek.

But the conquest of Canaan was not completed by the Israelites, either geographically or politically. The region was still part of the Egyptian empire, and important sections of the country, such as the coastal plain occupied by the Philistines, could not be resettled. Moreover, the twelve tribes then constituting Israel—each descended from a son of Jacob—divided and asserted their individual independence or formed loose and shifting confederations. Invasions of other nomadic peoples were a constant threat. Still, the "seed of Abraham" had returned—the first of several such historic homecomings.

Under their tribal rulers or "judges," the people of Israel settled down to life in Canaan as farmers and herdsmen. They traded with those master merchants of the ancient world, the Phoenicians. Some were attracted to the rich life of the cities, where they became craftsmen and mingled with other nationalities.

But the political disunity of Israel spelled military weakness—in that time, a clear invitation to destruction and enslavement. Especially menacing were the Philistines, a seafaring people originating in Crete and the Aegean Islands, who had built great cities along the Mediterranean coast. The Philistines were the first warriors to use weapons of iron; against the Israelite tribes they were invincible.

The disorganized Israelites, despite the heroic efforts of such leaders as Samson, were repeatedly defeated. In just one disastrous battle, at Aphek, they lost thirty thousand men—equal to the combined losses of the Union and Confederate armies at the Battle of Gettysburg! Israel was reduced to a land of subject people, and the conquered territory came to be known as Palestine—the Roman equivalent of "land of the Philistines."

Yet there was hope that a unified force might still drive out the invaders. The liberating army would have to be led by a strong commander—a king. The tribal leaders—notably Samuel, the last and greatest of the judges—chose Saul of the tribe of Benjamin to establish a monarchy.

A daring and skillful general, King Saul waged several successful campaigns against the Philistines. A memorable episode in one of the battles was the defeat of the Philistine champion, Goliath, by a young court favorite of Saul named David.

Later, David became such a popular hero that he aroused the envy of the king and was hunted as an outlaw. But with the death of Saul, David assumed the throne. Vigorously pursuing both foreign and domestic enemies, he eventually united all of Israel as an independent kingdom for the first time. He made Jerusalem his capital city, and it has ever since remained the national and religious center of the Jewish people.

Despite almost continuous warfare, David established a stable government in Israel. His descendants followed him to the throne, ruling for centuries and forming the only considerable dynasty in Jewish history. Warrior, statesman, and poet, King David is regarded as the founder of the Jewish state. And the Star of David is still the national symbol of Israel.

3 The Second
Thousand Years

The child of one of the world's most widely publicized romances, Solomon—son of David and Bathsheba—was destined to carry the ancient kingdom of Israel to the height of its glory. With the wisdom that has become legendary, Solomon extended the borders of the state and presided over a period of unusual peace and prosperity. The nation was strengthened by alliances formed with neighboring rulers and became a thriving commercial center.

Above all, King Solomon was a great builder. The most significant of his projects was the construction of the Great Temple in Jerusalem. It came to be regarded as the symbolic center of world Judaism, and its later destruction is still commemorated as the most tragic event in Jewish history. Even today, its site remains the holiest of places to practicing Jews.

This is a good point—during the years of Solomon's reign—to pause for a glance about the world of the time to see what was going on in other lands. In China, the Chou dynasty ruled a powerful empire in an era known as the Golden Age of Chinese culture. Many of the greatest Oriental poets and philosophers lived during this period.

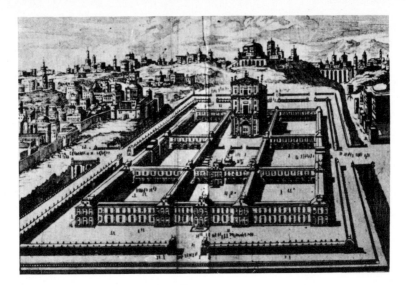

Illustration from an English Bible showing the elevation of the Temple of Jerusalem

The dedication of King Solomon's Temple

In India, the Aryan invasions had come to an end, and early Hindu civilization—later to become one of the world's most creative cultures—was taking root.

Closer to Israel, Greece was still in its archaic period, centuries away from the height of its influence. But a legendary blind poet, Homer, was already composing his epic poems, the *Iliad* and the *Odyssey*. Farther west in Italy, a semi-barbaric people, the Latins, had settled on seven hills near a river, at a place later to be known as the eternal city of Rome.

But then, in Israel, Solomon died, and his death signalized a period of decline. Dissension within the nation was renewed. Ten of the tribes seceded and formed an independent kingdom in the north, which—confusingly—was now to be called Israel. The remaining two tribes in the south continued to be ruled by the descendants of David as a kingdom called Judah. For two hundred years, the rival Jewish states uneasily coexisted.

Israel, the northern kingdom, unfortunately bordered on territories inhabited by powerful and warlike peoples. Under frequent attack by its neighbors, it was further weakened by continuous internal quarrels.

The Assyrian empire, then at its peak of strength and influence under King Sargon, soon found the northern kingdom an easy conquest. The imperial rulers of antiquity believed in total war; the defeated Israelites were made captive, transported to distant parts of the Assyrian domain, and scattered. Recorded history has nothing more to say of these ten tribes. They presumably were absorbed by the peoples they lived among, lost their identity as Jews, and disappeared. But speculation has persisted about the fate of the "Lost Tribes of Israel." At one time, a theory was even advanced that the American Indians were descended from them.

Judah, the southern kingdom, was able to remain independent for 115 years longer. Then another great ancient empire, the Babylonian, was enjoying an era of territorial expansion. In 586 B.C., Nebuchadnezzar, King of Babylon, invaded Judah and destroyed Solomon's Great Temple. This time the remaining two tribes were led into captivity in their turn.

And so, more than twenty-five hundred years ago, the entire land of Israel became a mere possession of a foreign power. Most of its people had vanished forever; the rest were held captive in exile. The Diaspora, or dispersion of the Jews, had begun.

By all that is known of the social sciences, it would have seemed likely that the Jewish nation would soon join the Hittites, the Sumerians, and the Chaldeans as just another ancient Near Eastern civilization which had briefly contributed to world culture but was now nothing more than a footnote to history. It might have seemed probable that, in our time, a few pieces of pottery in some museum would be all that was left of the Hebrews.

But the people of Israel, as they went into exile, took with them their Torah, their commandments, and the sacred writings of their prophets. "By the waters of Babylon" they longed for their ancestral home and kept faith with their traditions. The Babylonian captivity had the unexpected effect of unifying the Jewish exiles and strengthening their determination to preserve themselves as a nation.

About thirty years later, Babylon had run its course as a major world power and was replaced by the Persian empire. King Cyrus of Persia swept over the "fertile crescent" of Babylonia and Israel as well. Some of the original exiles from Judah were still alive to hear Cyrus say that they and their descendants were free to return to their homeland.

Once again, a great exodus took place as forty-two thousand Jews made their way back to the land of Israel. Still others joined them later in a migration that extended over a hundred-year period.

As a province of distant Persia, the Jewish state was granted a considerable measure of self-rule. In this period of national revival known as the Second Commonwealth, the Temple was rebuilt in 516 B.C., and the spiritual roots of the people became even firmer and deeper.

Alexander the Great, the conqueror who swept out of Greece to master most of the ancient world, defeated the Persians in 322 B.C. In another round of imperial musical chairs, Israel became a Greek possession, still retaining a large degree of self-government.

For well over four hundred years, then, the people of Israel continued to practice their religion in peace and to expand their cultural institutions. They lived, of course, in political subjection to two great empires, but their rulers were tolerant. The land prospered in peace and security.

But with the death of Alexander the Great, more difficult times came to pass. In an ironic commentary on the vanity of human ambition, Alexander's mighty empire promptly fell apart. Israel found itself under the domination of Syria.

Antiochus Epiphanes, the Syrian king, was a ruler determined to exercise complete mastery over his possessions. He was particularly bent on eliminating the practice of the Jewish religion. He defiled the Temple and other sacred places and persecuted those who clung to the faith of their ancestors.

Through the centuries, the Jews had been willing to abide some measure of imperial rule, but the harsh repression of the Syrian king proved unbearable. A revolt spread across the land from the hills of Judah, led by a priest named Mattathias and his sons, known as the Maccabees. Judah Maccabeus was the brilliant general who won a series of military victories against incredible odds: in one battle, for example, his hastily formed army of three thousand routed an enemy force of forty thousand men. He cleansed the Temple and restored freedom of worship. Simon, the youngest brother, became king, in 142 B.C., of a once-again independent state of Israel.

As has been observed, the early history of mankind abounds in battles which have been half-forgotten, but nevertheless resulted in the death of thousands. These ancient wars were most often motivated by a king's ambition for conquest and glory. But the revolt of the Maccabees, commemorated now in the Feast of Lights, or Chanukah, was the first war in recorded history for freedom of individual conscience. In a real sense, the Maccabees are the spiritual ancestors of the Pilgrims, of Roger Williams, and of the millions of anonymous Americans who similarly have held dear the basic human right to worship freely according to one's belief.

For two centuries, there was a period of national independence. At one point, the kingdom was restored to the territorial boundaries of King Solomon's reign. But then the Jewish state fell under the shadow of yet another great empire—the most powerful ever known—imperial Rome.

The Romans had not only fashioned the most efficient military machine in history, but they were admirably organized to administer subject peoples. Generally, they preferred to allow a local puppet king to act as a "front," while a governor sent from Rome, and supported by Roman armed might, held the real power and collected taxes.

Having enjoyed their freedom for two hundred years, the Jews were not inclined to submit easily to any new conqueror. Although Roman legions succeeded in occupying the country, guerrilla war —led by a band of patriots called the Zealots—was waged for more than one hundred years against the occupation forces. In 66 A.D., large-scale open warfare broke out in Israel.

For four years, this unimportant outpost of the mighty empire held off the battle-hardened imperial legions and outgeneralled a succession of skillful commanders sent from Rome. But in 70 A.D., Jerusalem fell, and the Temple was destroyed finally by the victorious Romans. Even so, for three years more, a dramatic last stand was made at the fortress of Masada.

Hundreds of thousands of Jews were killed or taken captive by the conquerors. Still the struggle was not abandoned. Another unsuccessful uprising occurred in 117 A.D. Led by the courageous Bar-Kochba, the Jews actually succeeded in defeating the Romans in 132 A.D. and driving them from Jerusalem.

Independence was regained, but only for a brief three years. Imperial Rome, controlling the world from far-off Britain to the borders of India, could not allow an upstart nation to set a pattern of rebellion that other peoples might follow. The Romans—accompanied at one point by their emperor, Hadrian—returned in greater force than ever. This time, with savage thoroughness, parts of the holy city of Jerusalem were completely leveled and buried, and its name obliterated. A temple to Jupiter was erected in the new Roman capital.

Leaving a scorched and ruined land behind them, much of the surviving Jewish population departed into exile or slavery, scattered throughout the vast reaches of the Roman empire. In the ages that followed, Israel became a remote memory.

4 Rebirth of a Nation

*A*lthough some small Jewish settlements did survive in Israel after the Roman conquest and have lasted until the present day, for nearly two thousand years most Jews lived far from the land of their origins. Meanwhile, other developments on the world scene soon added to the difficulties of these exiled people.

Christianity, a religion originating in Palestine during the Roman occupation, began to spread throughout the empire at just about the time of the dispersion of the Jews. By the end of the fourth century, it had become the official Roman faith. Eventually, all of Europe embraced the Christian creed.

Then Mohammed of Arabia founded the religion of Islam in the year 622, and it, too, rapidly gained millions of adherents, chiefly in Asia and Africa. Caught in the nutcracker of these two great religious movements, both militantly seeking converts, the Jews in exile faced an uncertain future in the early centuries of the Christian era.

As a people who resisted conversion and clung stubbornly to their own beliefs, the Jews of the time soon became the ready targets of suspicion and spiteful persecution. As a religious minority, in an era when church and state were closely linked, their rights as citizens were often limited, no matter where they lived. Because Jews seemed "different" in their non-conformity, popular ignorance, superstition, and envy were easily fanned into mob violence.

After the fall of the Roman Empire, Israel—once a "land of milk and honey"—became a neglected desert misruled by various foreign powers. Yet Jewish culture was kept alive in the cities of the Diaspora, or exile. For several centuries, Babylon was an important spiritual center. Then, after the year 1000, the most influential communities were to be found in western Europe.

Living among other peoples, Jews assumed diverse outward characteristics while retaining their own basic beliefs. Those Jewish communities which arose in Moslem countries came to be known as Sephardim. The height of their influence was reached in Spain in the twelfth and thirteenth centuries, when they made some truly remarkable contributions to literature and science. Some of the greatest names associated with this branch of Judaism are those of the philosopher Maimonides and the poets Ibn Gabirol and Judah Halevi.

The Jewish communities of northern Europe were called Ashkenazim. Through the Middle Ages, in the Christian nations of France, Germany, and Poland, these groups led a precarious existence, experiencing sharply alternating periods of ascendance and decline. Rashi, a French Jew of the twelfth century, is avidly studied for his brilliant commentaries on the Bible; in modern times, it has been this branch of world Jewry which has produced so many creative thinkers in the arts and sciences. Most American Jews, incidentally, stem from Ashkenazi communities.

In customs, language, and ritual, the differences which developed between the Sephardic and Ashkenazi groups have persisted until today. Yet, through the centuries of exile, each continued to

Moses Maimonides

cherish the memory of Israel as a homeland; both are represented in the population of Israel today.

When the chronicles of Europe in the Middle Ages are reviewed, certain major events stand out: the Crusades of the eleventh, twelfth, and thirteenth centuries; the Black Death of the fourteenth century; the Spanish Inquisition of the fifteenth. Each of these momentous occurrences has a special tragic significance in Jewish history; each meant mass murder, expulsion, and misery. Even at best, during this period Jews were barely tolerated and forced to live in crowded "ghettos"—dismal cities within cities.

Little wonder, then, that the vision of the Promised Land remained bright and beckoning. The believing Jew could draw comfort from his faith that the sacred soil of Israel was still his birthright; some day, he or his children would stand proudly as first-class citizens in their own country, own the land they lived on, and be privileged to serve as soldiers or statesmen.

And throughout the centuries of exile, small bands of Jews did manage to realize this dream and to find their way back to Israel. Both Judah Halevi and Maimonides made the long and dangerous journey; in 1211, three hundred French Jews were resettled. Still other groups came later, with the fall of the Byzantine Empire in 1453, and in flight from the Spanish Inquisition at about the time Columbus was discovering America.

With the development of political democracy in the seventeenth and eighteenth centuries, many Jews saw a more promising future in western Europe and America. The walls of the ghettos fell before the liberating influence of the French revolution; in Great Britain, Holland, and the Scandinavian countries, open societies offered fresh hope to the oppressed. And in America, from the beginning, Jews fought to build a new nation in which the persecutions of the past could be forgotten. To most Jews, the prospect of social equality and religious freedom—even as a small minority group—seemed preferable to vague longings for a land so legendary that it hardly had any real existence in the living present.

Typical of the "assimilated" Jew in this era of enlightenment was Theodor Herzl, a Viennese writer. Popular and successful, Herzl had no reason for misgivings about the gay, cosmopolitan life he enjoyed in the European capitals of the late nineteenth century. But in his capacity as a journalist, Herzl happened to "cover" the trial of Captain Alfred Dreyfus in France in 1895. Dreyfus, a Jewish military career officer, was the victim of an obvious frame-

Dr. Theodor Herzl

up motivated by anti-Jewish feeling and reactionary politics. He was convicted twice of espionage and treason until—after world-wide protests—he was declared innocent in a third trial.

The Dreyfus case made a profound impression on Herzl. He became convinced that the Jews would always be scapegoats like Captain Dreyfus so long as they were a defenseless minority. Herzl saw as the only solution the translation of an age-old dream into present reality—the reestablishment of a Jewish state and large-scale migration of the homeless. Through his speaking and writing, he promoted the movement called Zionism; he convened the First World Zionist Congress in 1897 in Basle, Switzerland.

Herzl's appeal evoked a ready response in a score of nations. Thousands of pioneers returned to the land of Israel, laboriously cultivating the desert soil, establishing industry, building new cities.

Within twenty years, eighty-five thousand Jews lived in Palestine, then under Turkish rule.

The outbreak of World War I presented the Zionists with an unexpected opportunity. Great Britain was eager to gain support in its conflict with Turkey over the Middle East. In 1917, the British government issued the Balfour Declaration, pledging establishment of a "national home" in Palestine. A legion of Jewish soldiers was formed under the British flag and took part in the fighting. Then, after the war, Britain was granted a "mandate" to act as the protector of Palestine so that the Jewish nation could be reconstructed.

The resettlement of Israel under the British mandate proceeded rapidly in the years that followed. By the time of the Second World War, the Jewish population had risen to 650,000. Nevertheless, on the eve of this greatest of wars, the practical possibility of immigration to Palestine seems to have appealed to only a small proportion of world Jewry.

Then came World War II. In the long history of the Jewish people, only broadly sketched in these chapters, no worse catastrophe is recorded than the genocide, or mass murder, committed by Germans led by their dictator, Adolf Hitler, during this period. Six million Jews were among the thirteen million Europeans of all faiths to be brutally killed—by gas, by torture, by barbarous "scientific" experiments. Even those who survived were often broken in mind and body. Scholars and thinkers are still trying to comprehend the madness which could lead whole nations to participate or even acquiesce in such systematic destruction of millions of human beings.

Jews both inside and outside of Europe fought back against the Hitlerite armies. Thirty thousand Jewish soldiers enlisted in

Palestine and formed a Jewish brigade, which saw action on several
European fronts. Hundreds of thousands of others served in the
ranks of Allied armies. Within the territories occupied by German
forces, many Jews joined underground resistance units and partisan bands. The battle of the Warsaw Ghetto—in which the pitiful
remnants of the once-great Jewish community of Poland for weeks
fought off a modern German army equipped with tanks and dive
bombers—must surely be counted one of the glorious triumphs of
the human spirit.

With the end of the war and the defeat of Germany, the surviving European Jews could not be expected to renew their lives
amid the ruins of their homes and the unmarked graves of friends
and families. Moreover, they could hardly face a confident future
among neighbors who had seen them off to death once before.
Israel seemed to promise an opportunity to reconstruct some sem-
blance of normal existence.

Even before World War II, however, Arab rulers in the Near
East had come to look upon the Jewish resettlement of Israel as
a threat to their dominant position in the region. During the war,
several Arab leaders collaborated with Hitler, hoping that a German victory would resolve their problem with the utter annihila-
tion of the Jews. Now the postwar flood of immigration strengthened Arab determination to halt the further growth of Jewish
communities in the area and to destroy the existing settlements.

The British administration proved unable to cope with the
difficulties posed by Jewish immigration and Arab opposition. The
British tried to limit the number of Jews who could enter; in turn,
they were harassed by guerrilla warfare and terrorist attacks between Arabs and Jews, both being dissatisfied. At last, in 1947,
Great Britain dropped the "Palestine Question" in the lap of the

United Nations. A special committee appointed to study the issue recommended that the British mandate be terminated and the territory in dispute be "partitioned" into two independent states, one Jewish and the other Arab. The UN Assembly approved the committee recommendation.

Although Jewish sentiment was not completely satisfied by the partition proposal, the plan was nevertheless accepted by the Jewish Agency for Palestine, representative body of the Jewish people under the mandate. The Arab nations, however, immediately announced they would fight the creation of any Jewish state by force of arms.

When the State of Israel was formally proclaimed on May 14, 1948, with the revered Chaim Weizmann as its first president, five Arab nations made war on the new government at once. But Israel was able to defend itself successfully, and armistice agreements were signed a year later.

Arab antagonism toward Israel extended to the Jewish communities long established within the Arab nations themselves. Jews in Asia and Africa, after having lived in peace within Arab societies for centuries, now found themselves the objects of harassment. Israel was the logical haven for fresh hundreds of thousands of immigrants from Iraq, Yemen, Morocco, Algeria, and other Arab states.

And the armistice, of course, did not end the state of war between Israel and her neighbors. Egypt used her control of the Suez Canal to blockade Israeli ports; outbreaks of violence along the six-hundred-mile Israeli frontier took thousands of lives. A threatening buildup of Arab armed might led to the Sinai campaign of 1956, in which Israeli units swept across the peninsula to the Suez Canal, clearing out the hostile military bases. A United

James G. McDonald, first U.S. Ambassador to Israel (left)
Dr. Chaim Weizmann, first President of Israel (center)
David Ben-Gurion, first Prime Minister of Israel (right)

Nations force was later sent into the region to police the troubled border and avert future conflict.

In 1966, frontier clashes with Syrian armed bands once again brought the Arab-Israeli problem to the attention of the United Nations. But by this time, Israel was a going concern; friendship with the emergent nations of Negro Africa paid off as Kenya and Uganda strongly and successfully supported the Israeli position before the Security Council. In any case, the Arab powers could certainly have no realistic expectation of sweeping the reborn nation into the sea. Nevertheless, in 1967 Egypt reaffirmed the

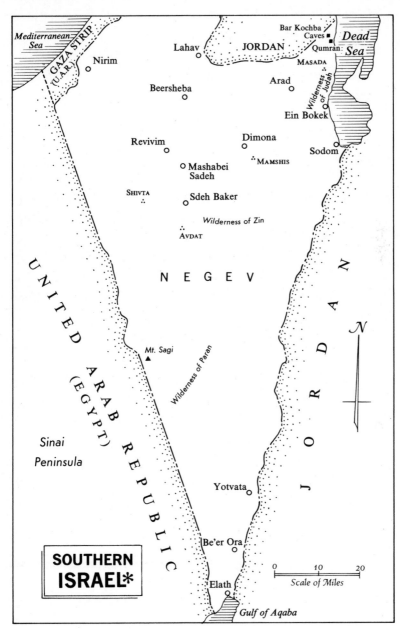

Mediterranean Sea

GAZA STRIP (U.A.R.)

Nirim

Lahav

JORDAN

Bar Kochba Caves

Qumran

Dead Sea

MASADA

Beersheba

Arad

Wilderness of Judah

Ein Bokek

Revivim

Dimona

Sodom

MAMSHIS

Mashabei Sadeh

SHIVTA

Sdeh Baker

Wilderness of Zin

AVDAT

N E G E V

U N I T E D   A R A B   (E G Y P T)   R E P U B L I C

Mt. Sagi

Wilderness of Paran

J O R D A N

N

Sinai Peninsula

Yotvata

SOUTHERN
ISRAEL*

Be'er Ora

Elath

0   10   20
Scale of Miles

Gulf of Aqaba

*See map, page 11, for areas taken by Israel in June, 1967.

state of belligerency with Israel, closing the Gulf of Aqaba to all shipping destined for the port of Eilat. At Egypt's request, the United Nations force was withdrawn from the border between the two countries and full-scale war broke out again. Syrian, Jordanian, Iraqi, and Egyptian forces—supported diplomatically by a host of other Arab and communist-bloc nations—were engaged against Israel.

A lightning six-day campaign followed in which Israeli armies fanned out across the Sinai peninsula to the Suez Canal, occupied strategic Sharm-el-Sheikh at the entrance to the Gulf of Aqaba, and took possession of the Gaza Strip, the west bank of the Jordan River, the Old City of Jerusalem and the heights along the Syrian border. Militarily, it was one of the most stunning victories in history; confident in their superiority in numbers of men under arms and equipment, the Arab ground and air forces were nevertheless utterly crushed by Israeli strategy, leadership, and morale.

A cease-fire was hastily arranged by the United Nations Security Council, which had previously been powerless to prevent the war. Subsequently, a special session of the General Assembly was called. The Arab nations and their Soviet-bloc supporters hoped the General Assembly would allow them to salvage some shred of prestige from the debacle, but the session ended inconclusively. World opinion was not swayed by the oratory of Arab spokesmen and Soviet Premier Aleksei Kosygin, and neutral commentators saw the session as an Israeli diplomatic victory.

Israel has assumed an important role on the world stage. Pope Paul VI made an unprecedented visit there in 1964; President Shazar of Israel toured the United States in 1966. Diplomatic relations were established with nearly all nations outside the Arab bloc; ambassadors were exchanged even with West Germany.

Pope Paul VI, on a visit to Israel in 1964

The population of the nation continued to grow as Israel showed a remarkable ability to accommodate as many as sixty thousand new arrivals each year. By the fact of their coming, these immigrants demonstrated their optimism and confidence in the future. Industry, agriculture, education, science, and the arts—each flourished in a place that had been a wasteland only two generations before.

With the perspective of four thousand years of history, an American observer might well wonder what lies in store now for the Jewish state. But the Israeli man in the street never questions a certainty: he knows that Israel is at last here to stay.

5 Inside Israel

*A*t 4:06 P.M., Friday, May 14, 1948, in a simple but solemn ceremony, David Ben-Gurion proclaimed the establishment of the State of Israel. Under heavy military guard, the then chairman of the People's Council read his proclamation to a small audience in a white, two-story art museum in the center of Tel Aviv.

This historic action, making real an ancient dream, originally had been scheduled for 11:00 P.M. It was later advanced to mid-afternoon to avoid conflict with the Sabbath, beginning at sundown. The proclamation document was then signed by thirty-seven of the leaders assembled. Thus, a new nation was created, transforming thousands of persons without a country into proud citizens, ending twenty-five years of British rule, and placing firmly in the past thousands of years of imperial subjugation.

The new state also brought parliamentary democracy to the Middle East, where feudal lords and military juntas had long ruled dictatorially. To many who never before had participated actively in politics, independence at last meant a voice in determining their own destinies.

Throughout Israel, people sang, danced, toasted the new

nation, and wept with joy. Liberty-loving folk everywhere sent their congratulations. Not even the knowledge that hostile forces on every border were poised for invasion could curb the festivities. The traditional national anthem, *Hatikvah,* echoed through the ancient land as differences of birth and circumstance were forgotten in the common bond of statehood.

The provisional government took its first official action immediately after it was formed. It revoked the British White Paper of 1939 restricting Jewish immigration and land purchase—measures that had effectively slowed the resettlement of Palestine.

As Israel's government took more permanent form, it was watched closely by friendly democratic states, as well as by its hostile Arab neighbors. A small country with no tradition of self-government, Israel soon evolved a simple, workable structure that affords full expression to a fiercely egalitarian and politically conscious population. Drawing on earlier European and American experiences in democracy, Israel's political system contains several innovations such as a single-house legislature and an eighteen-year-old voting age.

In the historic proclamation, the new state outlined its future course:

> The State of Israel will be open for Jewish immigration and for the in-gathering of the exiles; it will foster the development of the country for the benefit of all inhabitants; it will be based on freedom, justice and peace as envisaged by the prophets of Israel; it will ensure complete equality of social and political rights to all its inhabitants irrespective of religion, race or sex; it will guarantee freedom of religion, conscience, language, education and culture; it will safeguard the Holy Places of all religions; and it will be faithful to the principles of the Charter of the United Nations.

The first general election under the new government was held in January of the following year. Both Jews and Arabs went to the polls—many for the first time in their lives—to elect representatives to the Knesset, or parliament—Israel's lawmaking body.

The Knesset, like so many other features of modern Israel, has its roots in ancient history. The *Knesset Gedola*, or Great Synod, was the legislature of Judea at the time of the Second Temple, more than 2,000 years ago. Now, as then, it has 120 members; it is a unicameral or single-house parliament, unlike the lawmaking bodies of the United States and Great Britain, which are bi-cameral, having two houses.

Members of the Knesset serve four-year terms, unless they vote to dissolve and hold new elections earlier. They elect a speaker, whose functions are similar to those of the speaker of the House of Representatives in the United States or the speaker of the House of Commons in Great Britain. Together with seven deputy speakers representing the main political parties, he forms the Presidium. The Presidium, along with a house committee, regulates the proceedings of the legislative body.

For some sixteen years, the Knesset conducted the nation's business in a modest building originally intended as a bank. Before that, it met in a converted movie house in Tel Aviv. But now the parliament is housed in a stunning modern structure on a hillside in the western part of Jerusalem called Givat Ram, opposite the Israel Museum and the central government offices.

Unlike the President of the United States, the chief executive of Israel is not elected by the people. Instead, Israeli government is based on the concept of ministerial responsibility familiar to European democracies. The Knesset elects the President for a five-year term; he in turn selects a member of parliament to be prime minister, and the prime minister chooses other cabinet officers. As in the United States, the President appoints judges and diplomats, and he receives foreign emissaries to Israel. He grants pardons, commutes sentences, and countersigns laws.

The Knesset acts largely through nine standing committees, which consider laws after debate by the full house. The committees also hear reports from cabinet ministers and other high officials. Membership on the committees cuts across party lines.

Debates in the Knesset are conducted in Hebrew, but a simultaneous translation—as in the deliberations of the United Nations—is available to Arab members. These members address the house in Arabic, and a Hebrew translation is given by an official interpreter from the rostrum.

The most lively debates occur when the Knesset considers the nation's annual budget. The appropriations for each ministry are considered, and any member of the Knesset may question a cabi-

New home of the Knesset, or Parliament

net minister on the efficiency of his department. It is the duty of the minister to reply—if he can.

Day-to-day administration of the nation's affairs is in the hands of the sixteen cabinet officers. These officials—often called "the government"—are pledged to carry out the policies of the Knesset. If they do not, they may be given a vote of "no confidence" and must then resign.

As a new state, Israel is politically oriented. In towns and cities, rural colonies, frontier settlements, military garrisons, Arab villages, and Bedouin encampments, old and young demonstrate enlightened citizenship. Despite its small population and unity of national purpose, Israel has about a dozen rival political parties.

No single party has ever commanded a majority in the Knesset. As a result, every cabinet has been the product of a coalition or temporary alliance. Sometimes—as elsewhere in the world—politics comes up with strange combinations, and political alignments shift from election to election. Nevertheless, the young nation has achieved a high degree of stability in government.

The leading political party is the Mapai, or Israel Labor Party. Among the other major organizations are the Herut Movement, founded by the pre-independence fighting force, the Irgun; the Liberal Party, a merger of Progressive and General Zionists; and the National Religious Party. Then there are the Mapam, or United Workers' Party; the Achdut Ha'Avoda-Poalei Zion, or pioneering Zionists; the Communist Party of Israel; the Agudat Israel, which stands for strict Torah observance; the Poalei Agudat Israel, or religious workers' movement; Cooperation and Fraternity, representing Moslems and an Arabic sect, the Druses; and Progress and Development, a party of Moslems and Christians in Central Galilee.

Moslem woman voting in an Israeli election in Jaffa

Youthful Israelis are articulate political activists. Citizens over eighteen can vote, and nearly all do. Election day in Israel has a distinctive atmosphere; there are always thousands of immigrants voting for the first time, and the question of how their ballots will be cast lends an additional element of uncertainty to the outcome.

In the 1965 election, 1,244,706 persons—83 percent of the electorate—voted, a remarkable record of popular participation in the democratic process. In a recent presidential election in the United States, only 62 percent of the electorate went to the polls.

Despite the number of political parties, election campaigns in Israel are similar to those in democracies elsewhere in the world. The familiar hurly-burly of newspaper advertisements, posters, speeches, and talk at the dinner table, in barber shops, and in taxis is just as prevalent in Israel as in the United States. But an American visitor may be surprised at certain restrictions imposed by Israeli election laws: forbidden are entertainments to attract the public to political rallies; the use of loudspeakers except to amplify an orator's voice; distribution of food, drink, or gifts; filmed campaign appeals; and pictures of the candidates in the newsreels near election day. Each political party is given only twenty-five minutes of radio time plus four additional minutes for every seat it holds in the outgoing Knesset. (There is no nationwide TV in Israel yet.)

At seven o'clock on the evening before the election, the whole country falls politically silent. Voting starts at seven in the morning, when 2,500 polling places open. Ballots are then cast until midnight, when the counting begins. About 250,000 citizens take an active role in the electoral process, serving on election boards, at polling stations, or as party workers.

Israelis vote for a party, slate, or political philosophy rather than for individual candidates. The voter cannot split his ticket; he casts his ballot by selecting a slip with a party symbol on it, inserting it in an envelope, and then dropping the envelope into the ballot box.

Seats in the Knesset are awarded to the respective political parties in proportion to the votes cast in their favor. For example,

Election posters in Israel

if a single party or coalition wins 50 per cent of the total vote, it gets 60 of the 120 seats in the Knesset. The first sixty candidates on that party's list are declared elected, and so on down the list if an even greater proportion of the votes are won. Any party receiving at least 1 percent of the vote shares in the distribution of parliamentary seats. When a vacancy in the Knesset occurs through death or resignation, it is filled by the next man or woman on the appropriate party list.

In a recent election, forty-five seats went to the Alignment, a coalition of the Mapai and Achdut Ha'Avoda; twenty-six to the Gahal-Herut-Liberal bloc; eleven to the National Religious Party; ten to the Rafi or Israel Labor List, an offshoot of Mapai; and fewer than ten to each of nine other political organizations. The most interesting change in the composition of the Knesset in recent years has been that more of the legislators are men and women born in Israel or in Moslem countries; fewer have come from Europe.

In addition to the national government, Israel has a complete network of local authorities, elected every four years, which deals with matters such as schools, roads, sewage, sanitation, and social welfare. Towns have local councils according to their size, and smaller villages send representatives to regional bodies. There is widespread popular participation in "grass-roots" government; public representatives even sit on quasi-judicial commissions which consider rent disputes, appeals against tax assessments, and similar pleas.

One American observer, noting the proliferating political activity in Israel—its multiplicity of parties and the numbers of its citizens directly involved in the governing process—compared it to Lilliput, the ridiculous little country of *Gulliver's Travels* where numerous factions contest unimportant issues. Perhaps so, but a people long denied self-government may be pardoned if it takes rather seriously the right to speak up and act out its political convictions.

6 Meet the People

*I*srael's population of approximately 2,600,000 is more diverse than that of most larger nations. Combining the colors and qualities of a variety of mankind, like a patchwork quilt, the nation also has a unity that comes from the common thread of a capacity for sacrifice, a passion for freedom, and a centuries-old link with the Biblical past.

Israel's vast program of immigration, or the "in-gathering," has brought together people from all parts of the world. All told, about 1,250,000 immigrants have been settled on the land of their forefathers since independence.

Where did the young nation's immigrants come from? In the first eighteen months following the declaration of independence, 341,000 newcomers landed in Israel. Many were from the "displaced persons" camps of Germany and Austria or had been mustered out of wartime partisan bands and underground resistance armies—the survivors of Europe's Jewish communities after six million of their coreligionists had been destroyed.

Others came from Turkey, Bulgaria, and Yugoslavia. Some 5,000 refugees finally "made it" from Yemen after four years of

Yemenite Jew

homelessness in Aden. And all but 2,000 of the 32,000 Jews in Libya had gone to Israel by the end of 1951.

A total of 45,000 Yemenite Jews were taken out in "Operation Magic Carpet" in the eighteen months after May, 1949, when the Imam of Yemen at last permitted them to migrate. In one of the great humanitarian airlifts of modern times, these Yemenites, who had lived primitively under a despotic ruler, were flown to Israel in converted transport planes—fulfilling, for them, the ancient prophecy that they would one day return to their homeland "on the wings of eagles."

Five thousand Jews came out of China and 35,000 from Morocco, Algeria, and Tunisia. Others made their way from Poland, Romania, Hungary, Persia, and Iraq.

Today, the majority of immigrants no longer come from western Europe—or even eastern Europe—but from Asia and North Africa. Recent data place the number of new arrivals at 47,639 in 1961; 61,328 in 1962; 64,364 in 1963; and 54,716 in 1964. In 1965, the total fell sharply to 29,000, and in 1966 to a mere 17,000.

Since the immigration is not homogeneous, the newcomers speak a variety of languages and bring with them the habits of their native cultures. Oriental and Western Jews are often centuries apart in education and aspiration.

An American visitor to an Israeli city, village, or rural settlement finds it impossible to identify a reasonably representative national "type." He sees instead many people who resemble his friends and neighbors in the United States. Among the non-Jews, however, the Arabs in flowing robes and headcloths are an exotic element in the population; the more familiar Christian priests, monks, and nuns in the vestments of their religious orders also make a colorful sight.

Israel's population in pre-war 1967 included 2,240,000 Jews; 202,300 Moslems; 56,000 Christians; and 28,600 Druses and members of smaller sects. Native Israelis are called "Sabras," a name taken from the fruit of the cactus plant which is prickly outside but sweet inside. The image recalls the tough, unyielding exterior of the modern pioneer along with his inherent sense of compassion and social justice.

The country's population is becoming increasingly native in character. Recent statistics show that about 40 percent of the inhabitants were born in Israel; 31 percent in Europe and America; 15 percent in Africa; and 14 percent in Asia.

Government circles give much thought to the problems of cultural assimilation. For example, Moroccans from the caves of

Bedouin woman in kitchen in modern house

the Atlas Mountains in Africa must now be taught the rudiments of sanitation. Specially trained squads of girl leaders and teachers guide many of the North African immigrants through the mysteries of kitchens, toilets, sinks, and the simple amenities of modern housing.

Young Moroccans and other North Africans who take to the road for the first time in cars and motorcycles give Israeli police considerable difficulty because of their unfamiliarity with traffic rules and their inability or unwillingness to accept the discipline of local and state regulations. Progress is being made, however, and the slow process of building a unified nation moves forward.

In the diversity of the immigrant population also lies a strength only now beginning to be appreciated. Just as it did in the United States, the "melting pot" has brought out the potency and vitality inherent in many cultures.

Within the ranks of the European Jews there is a split that is as fresh today as it was a half-century ago. The pioneering, Zionist-oriented Europeans with a strong socialist tendency who built the communal settlements, staffed the underground armies, and formed progressive political parties are on one side. Statehood was long their aim, and they are often referred to as the Establishment of Israel.

The other faction is made up of groups of pious Jews from the same areas of eastern Europe. They form extreme orthodox reli-

The Mea Shearim, Orthodox Jewish quarter in Jerusalem

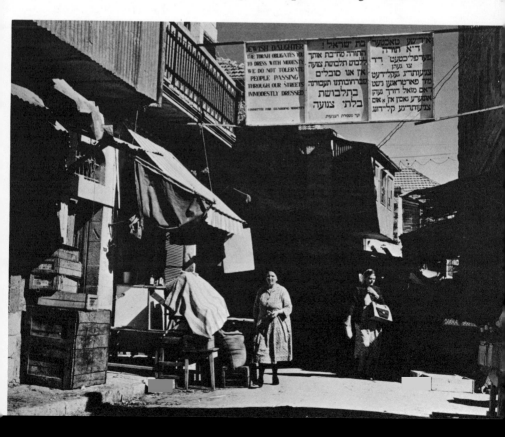

**Chassidic child of
the Mea Shearim**

gious sects and live in the Mea Shearim quarter of Jerusalem, in
Safad, or near B'nei Brak. These enclaves are the strongholds of a
way of life based on a strict interpretation of the Torah and Talmud.

To these groups, the world is rigid, closed, and uncompromis-
ing. They look with dismay at the modernity about them. On
occasion, they seek to influence public policy, and their demands
for complete observance of the Sabbath have become the subject
of official government discussion.

The "average" Israeli Jew is moderately devout. He takes his
ease beginning Friday afternoon. Husbands, sons, wives, brothers,
and sisters mark the advent of the Sabbath by purchasing sweets or
flowers as they make their way home before sundown. On Saturday, work halts; many Jews go to the synagogue or spend the day

as a family unit. But for most of Israeli youth, it is a day of recreation, devoted to swimming, hiking, or playing tennis.

While this conflict between the political Jew and the religious Jew persists, the rising generation of Sabras may well chart new directions. Among them are large numbers of "emancipated" youth, who do not consider themselves Europeans or Africans and who have no memory of religious persecution. They identify in the main with an Israeli rather than a Jewish consciousness, and for them Biblical associations do not have a poignancy as with the older Jews.

Israeli educators, for example, have become concerned over the apathy of youth toward the study of Jewish history. School officials are seeking ways to enliven the traditional subject and to explore parallels with modern problems.

As a nation in which immigration has been a major concern for two decades, Israel is now beginning to experience the pain of emigration as well. Some 160,000 of the more than 1,000,000 who came into the country later moved away to other lands. These emigrants have cited, as reasons for their leaving, the border clashes, the economic problems stemming from inflation, the unpleasant climate, an inability to learn the Hebrew language, and the difficulty of forming an allegiance to a new state.

Of those who emigrated, 22,203 returned to Israel between 1948 and 1965. Many of these returnees received government assistance in getting a new start—for the second time.

A particularly troublesome aspect of the emigration problem is the "brain drain." More than six thousand college graduates have left the country since 1948 for western Europe, Canada, and the United States. The lure of higher incomes and more comfortable living abroad is cited as the major reason for the departure

Arab stone house

of doctors and scientists. A special government agency has been given the task of wooing the expatriate scholars back home.

As has been pointed out, Israel is a Jewish state, and nine out of ten Israelis are Jews. But the Arabs of Israel—including, in religious practice, both Christians and Moslems—are a significant element in the population. Most of the Arabs who lived in Palestine under the British mandate moved to surrounding Arab countries during the fighting of 1948. Those who remained, as well as those who later returned, live as Israeli citizens alongside their Jewish neighbors.

Most of the Arab population is concentrated in the fertile Galilee region. The traditional flowing robes and headdresses of the men and the colorful, brightly printed, billowing gowns of the women—many of whom still wear the veil—stand out in the crowds near Jerusalem and Nazareth.

The small, cubelike stone houses of Arabs cling stubbornly to the sloping terrain, and all have windows and doorways trimmed in green or blue to ward off the evil spirits. But many Arab farmers and workers own automobiles and no longer go to market on donkeys. Many families have television sets and are the targets of propaganda broadcasts beamed from Egypt and Syria.

Arabs vote as Israeli citizens and hold public office. The Arabic language is used in parliament and on street signs and is evident everywhere. Arab children are in school, and public health stations have been opened in Arab sectors, bringing modern medicine in place of primitive healing techniques.

The Arab standard of living has risen steadily and is almost equal to that of the Jewish population. The average annual income of an Arab family in Nazareth is 7,000 Israeli pounds, or about $2,310; that of an average urban Jewish family is 7,360 Israeli pounds. The Arab income is higher than that of a Jewish immigrant family from Asia or Africa (6,600 Israeli pounds).

In an effort to achieve closer contact between Arabs and Jews, Arab villages are being "adopted" by Jewish rural settlements. Joint outings and exchange visits between the children are held.

In the area around Beersheba, where the broad Negev opens up, live the Bedouin tribes. These people are nomads, still moving from valley to hilltop and back with the seasons. They graze flocks of camels, sheep, and goats and live in low, black goatskin tents.

The Israeli government has sought to stabilize the Bedouins, to move them into permanent homes so that they can send their children to school, get proper medical attention, and care for their flocks. The effort continues, but there is resistance. Bedouin chieftains contend that their people have always wandered, and they cannot understand why they should not continue to move into the

Arabs on market day in Beersheba

valleys to escape the cold and up to the hilltops to catch the cool breezes in spring and summer. Still, some progress has been made in settling the nomadic Bedouins; some of their children are in school and at the university, and some families have been persuaded to move into new housing.

One of the most colorful minorities in Israel is the Druses, who live chiefly in the Galilee about Shefar 'am, east of Haifa. They are Arabic-speaking people who broke away from Islam in the eleventh century. In 1956, for the first time in their history, they were granted the status of an autonomous religious community by the national government.

The Druses are a fine, handsome, proud people, who fought well beside the Jews in the wars for independence. The tenets of their religion are a well-kept secret, but every year they make a pilgrimage to the tomb of Jethro, father-in-law of Moses, near the Horns of Hittim in the lower Galilee overlooking Tiberias.

Another interesting small group among Israel's people are the 1,200 Circassians who live in two villages in the Galilee—Kafr Kana and Rehaniya. They were brought to Palestine in the nineteenth century by Sultan Abdel Hamid II.

Just as the landscape of Israel consists of layer upon layer of stratified history going back to antiquity, so does the population contain strains introduced over thousands of years. But in both cases, something new is being built on so much that is old.

Druse chief

7 Kibbutz, Moshav, and Boom Town

Israel's success in agriculture is due in large measure to a distinctive sociological innovation—the kibbutz, or collective settlement. An ideological cousin to such early American communal experiments as Brook Farm and New Harmony, the kibbutz (plural, kibbutzim) grew out of the twin necessities for cultivation and defense of the land. It provided a pattern of village development which has enabled students and merchants, transformed into farmers, to renew the productivity of the exhausted, eroded soil.

Jewish agriculture was first revived in Palestine about ninety years ago with the foundation of two settlements, Petach Tikva in 1878 and Rishon-le-Zion in 1881. These were organized on the model of European peasant villages, in which each landholder lived in his own house and cultivated his own patch of earth. The early farmers concentrated on growing citrus fruits and wine grapes, helped in their cultivation of cash crops by the philanthropy of Baron de Rothschild. In some twenty years, about nineteen such villages, based on private operation, came into being and survived with only fair success.

In the first decade of the twentieth century, a new type of

Israeli farmer

hardy settler, more socially minded, arrived in the country with the second *aliyah* or wave of immigration. Ten young men and two young women were given a piece of land by the Zionist Organization in the Jordan Valley south of Lake Kinneret, and they began working it as a group, pooling their labor and earnings.

This was the first kibbutz. Known as Degania, it set the pattern for future development. Today, it is still a flourishing community, more than fifty-seven years old, the seed from which a network of 230 other kibbutzim has sprung.

Kibbutzim are home today for more than 85,000 Israeli citizens. At least one-third of all agricultural production in the country comes from land tilled by members of these settlements.

But the kibbutz is a facet of Israeli life more important than statistics can reveal. Based initially on the philosophical belief that

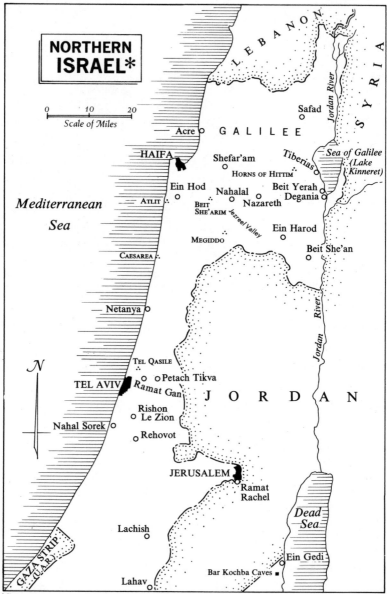

*See map, page 11, for areas taken by Israel in June, 1967.

Primitive hovels of the first kibbutz in Degania

a Jewish homeland can be achieved only when Jews are settled on the land, the kibbutz proved that an urban people could be trained to become efficient cultivators. Finally, it showed that stable, democratic communities could be organized without a profit motivation or property accumulation.

In other words, the kibbutz is not just a method of farming but a way of living. During Israel's early years, when border clashes were common occurrences, boundaries were best determined by actual settlement. Kibbutzim had the dual task of agricultural development and defense. While some members farmed, others guarded.

In the period between 1936 and 1945, the typical appearance of a kibbutz was that of a stockade with a watchtower, on the alert every hour of the day and night. Kibbutzim provided the early manpower cadres for the Hagana—a voluntary defense organization—and later for the Israeli army. Today, on the perimeter of Israel, kibbutzim still resemble armed outposts—fenced-in areas with powerful lights directed toward the border. Members of these kibbutzim carry arms and do regular patrol duty against infiltrators.

With the establishment of the state of Israel, and even in the provisional government before it, kibbutz members gained positions of national leadership. Many now hold high posts in the ministries, in parliament, in the defense forces, and in Histadrut, the General Federation of Labor.

What are the basic components of kibbutz life? A kibbutz is organized on the basis of complete equality, including the equality of all work. Every member is entitled to one vote, and the community as a whole decides on its course of action at a general meeting. This general meeting elects managerial personnel and the committees which deal with all aspects of life in the settlement. Election to a management position involves no special privileges.

The communal dining hall is the center of each kibbutz. Here, members meet three times a day to have their meals. Here, the general meetings take place, performances are given, and celebrations held. In the adjoining kitchen, food is prepared for all, and nearby there are laundry facilities, clothes stores, and the quarters of other artisans who care for the needs of the entire community.

Kibbutz members receive neither salary nor any other remuneration. Food, education, housing, health services, and vacations are free. Fixed sums are allowed for clothing and shoes. Cultural programs are provided, and all apartments have radios.

Children live apart from their families in their own quarters according to age group. They are cared for by housemothers. The youngsters join their parents when the workday has ended and spend afternoons and evenings with them. They attend school until the age of eighteen, when they enter the Army. They may in time become full-fledged members of the kibbutz on decision of the general assembly.

All assets and means of production in the kibbutz are communally owned. The main activities of kibbutzim are agricultural, but many have developed industrial branches, partly to process the products of the farming operations. Among these subsidiaries are plywood factories, handicraft production, light industries, and rest homes. Kibbutzim also hold shares in the National Bus Cooperative and have set up regional transport and fruit-packing cooperatives and factories.

But today the kibbutz is increasingly subject to critical examination: for the first time, its values are being questioned. With statehood and an effective military establishment a reality, the young native Israeli asks himself whether the rigorous life of the kibbutz is not in fact an anachronism. The kibbutz member, too, has been asking whether there is still need for the sacrifice and devotion to an ideal that made him give up the possibility of intimate family life for communal living. Still others wonder whether success has spoiled some of the more affluent kibbutzim.

The future of the kibbutz, therefore, has come in for some serious study in Israel, and it is on the agenda of the nation's new "think tank," a recently organized institute for the high-level consideration of non-military matters. Ironically, the institute is housed at Ramat Rachel, a once-flourishing kibbutz.

Some changes have already been made, not always to the satisfaction of the old-line kibbutz member. These include new housing

Present-day living quarters in kibbutz of Degania

providing greater privacy and comfort, increased mechanization
to reduce dull, tedious chores such as dish-washing, and the presence for the first time of beauticians for the women.

A recent poll among women members of the collective settlements indicates a sharp change in their outlook. Formerly, they
sought complete equality of the sexes. Kibbutz women always took
pride in doing any job a man could do. Today, they admit there
are distinctive feminine traits, and they are no longer sure of their
"equality"—or their desire to achieve it.

Sophisticated members of kibbutzim admit that it takes a special kind of person to be a good *kibbutznik*. Idealism is essential, and individual enterprise and initiative must be submerged or at least directed toward the communal good, with rewards secondary in importance. Critics of the kibbutz maintain that it is a refuge for the irresponsible man, for the individual who finds it difficult to make decisions and fit into the fabric of competitive society.

Members of the kibbutz often respond by explaining that the characteristic of equality extends to responsibility. A kibbutz member must share in the concern for the common good. If the member fails in this responsibility, he leaves or drifts away.

Among the thousands of new immigrants, the stickiest point about the kibbutz is family life, or maintaining the intimacy of husband, wife, and child as a social unit. A number of kibbutzim have taken cognizance of this aspect of the problem and have converted to family units in which the children now sleep at home.

A second type of farming village which developed successfully in Israel, largely as an outgrowth of this problem of family life in the kibbutz, is the moshav. The moshav is a cooperative workers' settlement based on mutual help, where every farmer nevertheless lives separately with his family and tills his own plot of land.

In the moshav, purchases and sales are made cooperatively by all members; heavy machinery is owned by the community as a whole. As in the kibbutz, the school, cultural center, and social services are maintained by the group, and the governing body is a general assembly of all members.

The first moshav was founded in 1921 by a dissident group from Degania on a swampy plot of land in the Valley of Jezreel,

A group of moshav children

west of Nazareth at Nahalal. This prototype of the moshav village
was designed in the shape of a wheel by planner Richard Kauf-
mann. The school, store, and other community buildings are
located at the hub, and the individual farms radiate out like spokes.
In the years following this moshav settlement, many moshavim
sprang up about the country. Today there are 367 such villages.

The moshav represents a compromise between the rigid cooperative structure of the kibbutzim and the private, unrestricted
farming pattern of villages such as Petach Tikva and Rishon-le-
Zion. Other variations developed, in time, to achieve a balance
between cooperative farming and individual family life; a third

type of settlement is the moshav-shetufi, which combined the collective-work principles of the kibbutz with the private-family system of the moshav.

In the cities—Tel Aviv, Haifa, Jerusalem—Israeli families live together in housing which may be primitive or spankingly modern, with terraces and up-to-date facilities. Here, factory workers, teachers, and merchants live much in the fashion of European and American middle-class families. Wealthy Israelis may live in handsome waterside or mountain villas. A vast housing program to rid the country of the old wooden and makeshift tin huts of an earlier time is now under way; consequently, newly arrived immi-

King David Boulevard in Tel Aviv

Some families still live in primitive, makeshift dwellings

grants from Asia and Africa often find themselves in modern apartments that confuse them.

In Eilat, the Red Sea port at the southernmost tip of Israel on the Gulf of Aqaba, and in Beersheba, the gateway to the Negev, life has some of the aspects of American frontier boom towns. Low buildings squatting on a dusty plain; the mixture of Asians, Africans, and Europeans; the jeeps, motorcycles, donkeys, camels, and goats; the tough, tanned soldiers and desert dwellers sweeping in and out on brief visits, add up to what has become the stereotype of frontier communities.

In Eilat, there is an imbalance between the male and female populations, just as was true in the American West and in Alaska. Single men live in special dormitories; married couples get private accommodations. Efforts are constantly being made to attract single girls from the north to this rapidly developing harbor city. Fortunately, there is little doubt that this situation will rectify itself in time.

At Beersheba, a city of some 70,000, growth has been spectacular. As the jumping-off place for the trek through the Negev to Eilat or intermediate points in the desert, the city is a bustling community. It has some Biblical significance as the site of Abraham's well, but perhaps of more interest to the visitor are a growing university, special laboratory projects on aridity, newly developed factories, large-scale housing, and mining operations in adjacent areas.

And so, in kibbutz, moshav, village, city, and frontier settlement, social organization in the new nation assumes a variety of forms. But there is one characteristic common to all life in Israel today—it doesn't stand still.

Motel in Beersheba

8 Going to School in Israel

To the youth of Israel, going to school is no more enjoyable than it is to boys and girls of other nations. But even the most reluctant scholar realizes that in Israel—more than elsewhere—education is an essential of survival.

Outnumbered thirty to one by hostile neighbors, living in a land with limited natural resources, the people of Israel understand that modern technology must be made their ally. Various agencies of the state, including the armed forces, are deeply involved in the urgent tasks of education.

Just consider the dimensions of the job that had to be done from the outset. Millions of immigrants had to be taught a common language, and cultural differences brought from seventy countries all over the world had to be bridged. In addition, a rapidly growing resident population had to be provided with schooling. And, as with everything in Israel, there was so little time, with the nation in a constant state of war.

Fortunately, there were materials at hand for building a superb educational system in the new nation. Devotion to learning is an ancient Jewish tradition, and there were a considerable number of well-educated men and women among the settlers of Israel.

While other newly independent states of Africa and Asia have had to create a professional class, Israel began national life with a fair supply of doctors, teachers, and lawyers, chiefly from Europe. But the expanding population and successive waves of immigration from the less-developed countries of the Middle East soon outpaced the services that this small corps could provide.

There was also a need for training in skills not readily available. Because of historical factors, there were few agricultural experts, veterinarians, metallurgists, and industrial engineers among the new arrivals to the young nation.

When Israel became independent in 1948, one hundred thousand young people were already attending school. But education was neither altogether free nor compulsory, as in the United States. Since that time, however, a Compulsory Education Law (1949) has been passed, and the school population has increased seven times over, compared with only a fourfold increase in the general population.

In the early years of statehood, many boys and girls attended school under conditions reminiscent of the American frontier. Classes were taught in tin huts and in tents, with students seated on the ground or on wooden planks. But new schools were rapidly constructed so that now all classes are held in regular buildings, even though some of the younger children must attend school late in the afternoon because of limited facilities.

The shortage of teachers was a major problem for the infant nation. For a while, the need was so great that almost anyone could be a teacher; there were no formal requirements. But gradually, teachers' colleges were established, and new, better-qualified teachers were trained while some of the older group were retrained. In fact, to encourage more men and women to become teachers, the

Army allowed its soldiers to attend evening courses in teacher-training institutions. From five thousand teachers in 1948, the corps of instructors in Israel has grown to more than thirty thousand. And all teachers must now be college graduates, while those who teach on a secondary level must have a master's degree.

The task of making Hebrew a living, national language for the diverse population was attacked on many levels. Young children rapidly learned the new tongue in communicating with each other; then they would take their knowledge of Hebrew home to the parents. An adult education program, often held at night, provided instruction for older people. The Israel Defense Army taught the language to young men and women in military service.

Classroom in a kibbutz school

Without this intensive campaign, Israel might have remained a mere illusion, a nation in name only, split into dozens of communities lacking a ready medium of communication. It would have been impossible, for example, even to give effective orders to the soldiers in the armed forces. Only through Hebrew—the language of their common prayers—could Jewish people from many lands be welded into an informed, alert citizenry owing allegiance to a nation which did not even exist a generation ago.

In Israel today, all children must attend school from the age of five to fourteen. Unlike American youngsters, they go to school six days a week. After this period of elementary education, what in American is called "high school" is neither tax-supported nor obligatory. Yet the period of compulsory, free education in Israel is comparable to that in progressive European nations and far in advance of neighboring Middle Eastern countries.

The most dramatic progress has been made in the schooling of Arab youngsters. Nearly all Arab boys now attend school, and 70 percent of the girls are in classrooms as well. They may attend schools in which the teaching is in Hebrew or those in which their native Arabic is the language of instruction.

Before the establishment of the state of Israel, education was a privilege denied to most Arab boys, and Arab girls almost never went to school. Even in the Arab nations of today, education is still a luxury available only to a fortunate few.

All schools in Israel are under the supervision of the Ministry of Education and Culture. Parents may enroll their children in any one of three kinds of schools. There are "state schools" and "state religious schools," both of which are entirely tax-supported. In the "state schools," children receive a secular or essentially non-religious education; in the "state religious schools" orthodox Juda-

Classroom in the Arab secondary school at Tirah

ism is taught along with the conventional subjects. Finally, there
are "recognized schools" operated by various organizations which
receive only partial government support. Most Israelis—about two-
thirds of them—prefer to send their children to the "state schools."

As is generally true in the United States, kindergarten is the
beginning of the Israeli child's education. Many three- and four-
year-olds go to kindergarten, but attendance is not compulsory
until the age of five. Then the youngster proceeds through the elementary grades, taking most of the subjects familiar to American
students. But there is considerable stress on agriculture and the
handicrafts, and, from the sixth year of study on, pupils take English, French, or Arabic as a second language.

Facing the same problem as American urban centers—the education of "disadvantaged" youth—the schools of Israel have made special provision for immigrants from the backward countries of Asia and North Africa. "Compensatory" education is offered through smaller classes and a longer school day. With this additional preparation, it is hoped that young people from underdeveloped areas will be able to compete more successfully with the students of European descent.

Of course, after-school activities are important to the Israeli boy and girl. Young people often join youth clubs, and during the summer vacations many go to camp. The Ministry of Education and Culture operates some of these summer camps with government funds.

Having completed the elementary course, young people between the ages of fourteen and eighteen may continue their education at general, vocational, or agricultural secondary schools, often paying tuition but sometimes obtaining financial support from municipal or town governments or private organizations. Most boys and girls choose to go to the general school. There are also certain special schools, such as the one which combines a secondary education with naval training for boys who wish to prepare for careers as officers in the merchant marine and navy. After completing this stage in their schooling, ambitious young people "sit" for matriculation examinations in order to gain admission to colleges and universities.

Higher education, as in America, is increasingly specialized. There are, for example, thirteen schools of nursing and numerous teachers' colleges. There are also schools of music and the other arts, preparing youth for careers with such renowned organizations as the Israel Philharmonic Orchestra and the Habimah theatrical company. Private talmudical colleges train young men for the clergy.

Two great universities form the apex of the educational pyramid in Israel. The Hebrew University in Jerusalem and the Israel Institute of Technology or "Technion" have been in existence since pre-independence days. Highly regarded in academic circles throughout the world, they have experienced an almost incredible expansion. In 1948, for example, the Hebrew University had just 900 students; fifteen years later the number had grown to 8,600. Professional training in a variety of fields, including the humanities, medicine, law, agriculture, and social sciences—as well as Asian and African studies—is offered at the Hebrew University.

Hebrew University, Jerusalem

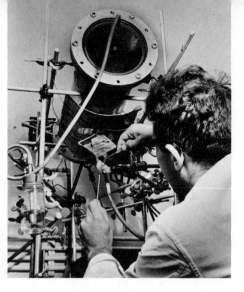

Experimental
physics research
at the Weizmann
Institute

Technion enrolls students in such technical courses as aeronautics, architecture, mining, and electrical engineering.

Advanced research is conducted at the Weizmann Institute of Science in Rehovot. Named for the famed chemist who became Israel's first president, the institute is engaged in work on a postgraduate level in such areas as nuclear physics, microbiology, and electronics. Many foreign students have come to the Weizmann Institute to study, and many Americans have contributed to its support.

The growing desire for higher education has led to the construction of new college facilities. Some recent additions are Tel Aviv University and Bar-Ilan University in Ramat Gan, founded by an American organization.

In any case, education in Israel—from the kindergarten to the atomic reactor laboratory—has a clearly defined aim. In the words of the State Education Law, the schools of the nation are dedicated to the achievement of "a society built on freedom, equality, tolerance, mutual help, and love of mankind."

9 A Language for a People

*I*f King Solomon had written a message and left it in a time capsule three thousand years ago, it could be read and understood by the Israelis of today. For the language spoken now in the narrow streets of Jerusalem is the same as the one that echoed in those very byways in Biblical times.

Like so much else in Israel, the survival of ancient Hebrew as a medium of communication goes counter to all the expectations of modern science—philology, in this instance. Once again, Israel is the exceptional case: to the man of faith a miracle, and to the unbeliever simply a freak of history.

According to the principles of linguistic development, language usage changes with time, and altered forms of expression gradually emerge. That is why the tales of Chaucer and even the plays of Shakespeare sound so strange to the English-speaking student of today. Eventually, the older language becomes still further removed from daily use and finally altogether unintelligible. It may then be called "dead," existing only in its literary or fossilized form, never again to be the vehicle of common speech.

And so the languages spoken elsewhere in the ancient world at the time Solomon built the Great Temple are now mere curious inscriptions in stone. Even the later ancient Greek and Latin are known only to scholars and priests. And yet Hebrew—the language of the Bible—still spells out today's newspaper headlines!

Actually, Hebrew probably did not originate with the Jews. An ancient form of the language was, in all likelihood, spoken in Canaan before the time of Abraham. Yet it did become the language of Israel and remained in use for fourteen hundred years. Not only the Old Testament but many great works of philosophy and ethics, such as the *Mishnah,* were written in Hebrew.

With the destruction of Judea by the Romans and the dispersion of the Jews in 135 A.D., Hebrew ceased to be a language used in everyday conversation. In order to conduct their daily affairs, the Jews of the Diaspora naturally learned the language of the countries in which they lived.

But the ability to speak Hebrew was not lost. In keeping with the Biblical injunction to teach the Torah or law "diligently unto thy children," the Jews continued, century after century, to instruct each generation in the ancient tongue. It remained, of course, the language of prayer and served as a medium of communication between Jews of different countries, often facilitating intricate international commercial arrangements quite remarkable for those days.

And Hebrew showed continued vitality as a literary language; the Jews of Spain composed great poetry in Hebrew, and for centuries it served the communities of France and Germany as the sole means of written communication. During the Middle Ages, when even kings were illiterate, virtually every Jew knew both Hebrew and the language of the country, and could read and write the ancient tongue as well.

In time, the restricted ghetto environment gave rise to other distinctive Jewish vernaculars: Yiddish, a form of medieval German, and Ladino, an offshoot of medieval Spanish. Although these languages developed rich literatures of their own, in the eighteenth and nineteenth centuries there was an increased production of poetry, plays, novels, and scientific works in Hebrew. The first Hebrew newspaper, a weekly called *Ha-Maggid,* appeared in 1856.

With the development of Zionism, the political significance of Hebrew as a unifying element in the reconstruction of a Jewish state was immediately grasped. Around the turn of the twentieth century, a host of gifted authors contributed to the flowering of

Chaim Bialik

Eliezer Ben-Yehuda

a modern literary Hebrew. At least one of them, the poet Chaim
Bialik, may justly claim a lasting place in world literature.

The Irish Renaissance, at about the same period, similarly
revived Gaelic as part of a national reawakening. Proposals to
reintroduce Sanskrit as a unifying factor in the multi-lingual nation
of India have also been advanced. But Hebrew is distinctive in
being an instance more of survival than revival.

Perhaps most instrumental in the practical application of
Hebrew to modern everyday life was Eliezer Ben-Yehuda (1858-
1922). An ardent Zionist, Ben-Yehuda foresaw that a reconsti-
tuted Jewish state would need a language of its own. On his way to
Palestine in 1880, he predicted: "Today we are speaking foreign
languages; tomorrow we shall speak Hebrew." In fact, on the ship
from Marseilles to Jaffa, Ben-Yehuda would address his wife only
in Hebrew; his son, born two years later, was the first child in modern times to be brought up with Hebrew as a primary language.

Ben-Yehuda understood that the schools of Israel would first
have to accept Hebrew as the language of instruction before it
could become a national language. A spirited campaign led, in
1892, to the decision of teachers from schools throughout the
country to use Hebrew exclusively. When Technion was founded,
in 1913, it was originally planned to teach the technical subjects
in German—a language particularly rich in technical literature—
but thousands of teachers and students went on strike, refusing to
return to classrooms until Hebrew was substituted.

During the period of the British mandate, Hebrew as well as
English and Arabic was given official status in law, postal service,
and government administration. But each wave of immigration
brought thousands of arrivals understandably reluctant to learn a
new language. Even so, by the time Israel won its independence in
1948, 80 percent of the population could speak Hebrew, and more
than half of them customarily used no other language. Today,
virtually all the people of Israel, including much of the Arab population, conduct their daily business in Hebrew.

Teaching the millions of immigrants to converse in Hebrew
was a truly remarkable feat of adult education. While children
readily picked up the language of their schoolmates, older people
had to be patiently taught—even while they were making painful
adjustments to new homes and new kinds of work in a nation living
in a virtual state of siege. To many, giving up accustomed patterns
of speech symbolized a turning-away from the family, friends, and
associations of the lands of their birth.

New methods of teaching language quickly were developed.
The *Ulpan* institutions were most effective, offering an intensive
five-month course to thousands of adults. Still another program
utilized volunteer teachers who went into homes and instructed

entire families in Hebrew. An "Easy Hebrew" vocabulary of a thousand words—similar to Basic English—was derived to provide an immediate working knowledge of the tongue to immigrants.

Hebrew is not much like any other language spoken in the modern world, and, for many immigrants to Israel, it posed special difficulty. The languages of the West are almost all members of the Indo-European family, derived largely from ancient Sanskrit. Hebrew, on the other hand, is a Semitic language, akin to such long-vanished ancient tongues as the Phoenician, the Edomite, and the Moabite. A distant modern relative—particularly in its sound system—is Arabic.

Unlike English, for example, Hebrew is read from right to left. It has an alphabet of twenty-two consonants quite different in appearance from English letters. Vowel sounds have no alphabetical symbols, but are denoted by ten possible patterns of "vowel points" which are usually omitted in material prepared for skilled readers. ·

Hebrew words are formed by adding prefixes and suffixes to certain roots, usually consisting of just three letters, or by changing the vowel sounds of those roots. The language is particularly deficient in the adjectives and adverbs which lend such richness to English expression.

It is understandable, therefore, that ancient Hebrew required some retooling to meet the demands of the atomic age. The Old Testament contains only 7,704 different words; modern life calls for a far more extensive vocabulary. Ben-Yehuda took the first steps toward compiling a Hebrew dictionary, but since 1904, the burden of fitting the language to the current scene has fallen chiefly on the Language Council—later called the Academy—and its numerous subcommittees. The Academy has published dictionaries of musical terms, of automotive phraseology, and of telephonic communication.

When words are needed for some contemporary purpose, the Academy locates the appropriate ancient Hebrew terms or compounds. Its pronouncements are binding on all official agencies and are accepted by scholars and writers. The Israel Defense Forces have a language committee of their own, to decide how instructions concerning modern weapons of war are to be conveyed in a three-thousand-year-old speech.

Some of the modern coinages have interesting derivations. For example, "garage" is *musach*—a word used in the Bible for part of King Solomon's palace; "newspaper" is *iton*—a derivative from the ancient Hebrew meaning "timely"; an ordinary match is *gafrur* or "sulphur"—the brimstone, according to the account in Genesis, rained upon Sodom and Gomorrah.

In the many countries of the dispersion, the pronunciation of Hebrew had undergone considerable change and variation. Speech patterns in the modern state of Israel had to be standardized to assure communication between people of different backgrounds. The traditional Sephardic pronunciation has been largely adopted as being closest to the speech of Biblical times.

The decision to make Hebrew the language of the new state has had certain disadvantages. Despite its rich literary tradition, Hebrew has the built-in handicap of being the speech of a small population, with not many more native speakers than Albanian or Latvian or Welsh. For this reason, nearly all Israelis know at least one other language, with English the favored second tongue. Obtaining textbooks in Hebrew for many school subjects, particularly in technical fields, has also been a major problem.

Still, Israel is a land where dozens of languages may be read and heard. Arabic enjoys a special status as the native tongue of more than 10 percent of the population, while there are daily newspapers in English, French, German, Russian, Polish, Ladino, Hungarian, Romanian, and Bulgarian as well. Yiddish, formerly scorned by many Israelis as a relic of the Eastern European ghettos, is now highly regarded, and the Yiddish theater is especially popular. In fact, courses in Yiddish language and literature are taught at Hebrew University.

But, in retrospect, there was really no alternative to the full adoption of Hebrew by the young nation. It was part of the heritage of Israel, and no other language could have won the acceptance of the millions of immigrants from greatly diverse cultures.

The outpouring of plays, films, and songs written in Hebrew testifies to the validity and vitality of the language today. In 1966, the greatest living Hebrew author, S. Y. Agnon, was awarded the coveted Nobel Prize. The language of the Bible has survived to take the form of a masterwork of modern literature.

10 New Nation, New Culture

A nation taught by its prophets that "man doth not live by bread only"—nor by technology, agriculture, or industry—Israel has experienced a dramatic cultural renaissance in the course of its brief existence. In a development which has historic parallels among other peoples, national independence brought a release of creative energy which has found new levels of expression in the lively arts, as well as in literature, painting, and sculpture.

Life in Israel today is, of course, a serious matter, and certainly its people have had their share of trial and tragedy; yet the country —judged by many criteria—is one of the most pleasure-loving in the world. For example, Israelis are probably the world's champion movie-goers, viewing an average of eighteen films a year per person. There are nearly three hundred movie houses where American pictures are the favorite offerings, accounting for more than half the films exhibited in Israel.

Cinematography, as an art and as an industry, has therefore become understandably important. An increasing number of full-length features, as well as many television programs and documentaries, are now being "shot" in Israel. Such Israeli productions as *Impossible on Saturday* and *Sallah* were well received by American critics and audiences.

Television, which accounts for so much of the average American's leisure time, is still in its infancy in Israel. The Columbia Broadcasting System of the United States, however, has been aiding in the development of TV operations in the new nation. Educational television has already been introduced in the schools of Israel, indicating the high priority given to instructional improvements.

As in Great Britain, radio broadcasting is conducted under government authority—meaning that there are no commercials. The Voice of Israel operates on thirteen wavelengths, broadcasting programs in the many native languages of its listeners, as well as in Hebrew. One radio station is devoted entirely to programs in Arabic and enjoys an audience throughout the Near East.

Of course, Israelis love the theater, and there are often as many plays being shown in Tel Aviv as on Broadway in New York. Many of the productions are original Hebrew works, but imports from the New York stage are highly popular. Musicals like *My Fair Lady* and *Fiddler on the Roof* have been successfully produced in Israel, while such serious dramas of American life as Edward Albee's *Who's Afraid of Virginia Woolf?* and James Baldwin's *Blues for Mr. Charlie* were theatrically effective in translation.

For American students of the theater who often complain of the commercialization of the Broadway stage, the Israeli repertory companies hold special interest. Habimah is the national theater, organized in Russia in 1918, but transplanted to Israel in 1928. It has frequently toured the United States, presenting classical dramas in Hebrew. Two other outstanding repertory groups are

Frederic Mann Auditorium in Tel Aviv

Ohel, founded as a workers' theater in 1925, and the Kameri Theater, established in 1944. These three companies are cooperative groups, managed by their actor-members and performing in their own theaters.

Aspiring young actors and actresses among Israeli youth may study in the Theater Arts Department of the Tel Aviv University or at Ramat Gan's Advanced School of Dramatic Art, founded by the Ministry of Education and Culture. And there are about two hundred amateur theatrical groups for those who love to perform as an avocation, as well as drama circles associated with schools and other organizations.

Music is another important aspect of the cultural rebirth of the nation. The Israel Philharmonic Orchestra is one of the world's leading musical organizations, boasting nearly thirty thousand subscribers—an international record, in proportion to population.

Such outstanding American artists as Leonard Bernstein, Artur Rubinstein, and Van Cliburn have appeared with the orchestra as guest conductors or soloists, both in Israel and on tours abroad. Its home base, the imposing Frederic R. Mann Auditorium in Tel Aviv, was built by an American.

An ancient Roman theater at Caesarea is now used for annual music festivals, at which such artists as Pablo Casals have performed.

American philanthropy has also been helpful in promoting musical education. Four centers have been established by the Americans for a Music Library in Israel, an organization which has also supported numerous school orchestras and choirs. The

Isaac Stern, Leonard Rose, and Eugene Istomin at Caesarea

American-Israel Cultural Foundation subsidizes various musical activities as well.

The dance, utilizing both classical and native themes, has many devotees. The Inbal Dance Theater, a troupe founded to preserve the folk art of the Yemenite Jews, was particularly appreciated by American audiences when it toured the United States some years ago.

Creative Israeli artists have produced a body of painting and sculpture which has earned high critical praise. Much of this art originates in the village of Ein Hod near Haifa, a settlement run by artists themselves, which has come to be known as one of the world's centers of creative expression. Another popular artists' colony has been established at Safad.

The role of the artist in Israel—particularly in the kibbutzim or collective farms, where hard manual labor is required of all—is still not fully resolved. If artists were to be given special consideration, leaving the arduous work to other members of the group, they could prove an irritant in a communal setting. Nevertheless, in many settlements artist-members are freed, by general agreement, from community work for part of the day so that they may devote themselves to individual creative activity. Some kibbutzim have their own art galleries, where exhibits and seminars are held.

Many of the art centers in Israel bear names testifying to American generosity. The Billy Rose Art Garden of modern sculpture in Jerusalem was a gift of the famed showman, while the Helena Rubinstein Pavilion in Tel Aviv was established by the noted cosmetologist. The Samuel Bronfman Biblical and Archeological Museum in Jerusalem was financed by a prominent Canadian industrialist.

There are scores of art museums scattered through the country,

Artists' colony at Ein Hod

several of them devoted solely to modern art. The newest and largest is the Israel Museum in Jerusalem, which includes the Bezalel Museum of Jewish folk art. The Bezalel School enjoys great prestige as a training ground for young artists.

Israelis are avid readers, and there are twenty-five daily news-papers—sixteen in Hebrew and the others in a variety of languages. An American visitor to Israel would probably find himself reading the *Jerusalem Post,* an English-language daily established in 1932. All shades of political opinion are represented in the press, which of course enjoys great freedom of expression.

There are about four hundred other periodicals in the small country, chiefly weekly and monthly publications. The Associated Israeli Press serves the same function as the American Associated Press; a Government Press Office is the official liaison with news-gathering media.

Some two thousand books a year are published in Israel, and thousands of volumes are imported from the United States and other nations, making Israelis one of the "readingest" people in the world, according to UNESCO figures. There are over a thousand libraries throughout the country with eight million books on their shelves. The largest is the Jewish National and Hebrew University Library in Jerusalem, containing a million volumes.

Nobel prizewinner S. Y. Agnon, who delivered his laureate address in Hebrew before King Gustav Adolph and the masters of the Swedish Academy, concluded his speech with a prayer: "May the earth be filled with knowledge and with joy everlasting to all its inhabitants, and may they take pleasure in peace abundant."

Agnon's work is an interesting amalgam of old and new. Pro-foundly influenced by traditional Hebrew literature—the Bible, the *Mishnah,* the Talmud, and Rashi's commentaries—Agnon's

The King of Sweden applauding S. Y. Agnon at Nobel
Prize ceremony in Stockholm

fiction is, at the same time, rich in the symbolism and psychological
analysis so characteristic of modern writing. Several of his novels
and shorter works are available in English translation: *The Bridal
Canopy* (1937), *The Days of Awe* (1948), *In the Heart of the
Seas* (1948).

Other noted Israeli authors whose work may be read in English
are Uri Zvi Greenberg (*Jerusalem,* 1939) and Aharon Megged
(*Hedva and I,* 1957). The poets Nathan Alterman and Abraham
Shlonsky are highly influential figures whose verse has also been
translated.

Each year, the national government awards the Israel Prizes—
equivalent to America's Pulitzer Prizes—to outstanding scholars,
artists, scientists, and writers. At least fifteen other literary awards
are made annually as well, including the Tel Aviv Bialik Prize to

commemorate Chaim Bialik, the greatest of modern Hebrew poets, who died in 1934.

As the "people of the Book," Israelis are eager students of the Old Testament. The Israel Society for Biblical Research sponsors lectures and study circles and publishes a quarterly review. In fact, the senior study circle of the society is headed by President Zalman Shazar. Popular interest in Biblical research is manifested in local quiz contests, which culminate in a national competition leading to the selection of an Israeli champion. Also, an International Bible Contest, presided over by a jury of eminent Christian and Jewish authorities, is held in Jerusalem with entrants from many nations, including the United States. A Seventh Day Adventist won a recent world championship.

Sports have a place in the Israeli cultural scene as well. Unlike the United States, Israel has no professional athletes; even its top-notch players hold full-time jobs generally unrelated to athletic competition. The favorite team sport is soccer, with important games drawing as many as seventy thousand spectators. Basketball has become increasingly popular, however, in recent years; even small settlements have their own basketball courts.

The climate of Israel is well suited to year-round outdoor sports activities. A long-distance swimming race across the Sea of Galilee is a popular annual event, while skin diving and water skiing have a growing number of adherents. A new golf course at Caesarea has attracted a membership of nearly a thousand.

The most important center for physical education is the Wingate Institute of Physical Culture, named for General Orde Wingate, a British military leader strongly sympathetic to Israel's national aspirations. Physical-training instructors from other Asian and African countries have attended courses at this institute.

Israel has participated in the Olympic games since 1952 and enters teams in other international tourneys, such as the Davis cup competition in tennis. But for Israelis, the Maccabiah games, in which Jewish athletes from all over the world compete, are perhaps more rich in sentiment. Held every four years—but not in conflict with the Olympics—the games attract more than a thousand athletes from scores of countries, including the United States.

In 12 B.C., Jewish athletes first competed in the stadium of Caesarea—on the very site of the modern golf course. Some things have not changed much in Israel, even in two thousand years.

11 Israel at the Ready

*A*s close students of their own history, the leaders of Israel have learned some of its military lessons well. The way the new nation has handled its defense problems since the proclamation of statehood provides a model for programs in Latin America and in several of the newly developing nations of Africa.

At the time it declared its independence, Israel already had at hand the voluntary defense organization, the Hagana, and several other fighting forces which had operated as underground armies. Some thirty thousand men and women serving in these illegal battalions originally received their basic training with the British in World War II. In the underground forces, they became particularly proficient in the use of small arms and learned to function in small, independent units.

Only a few minutes after it attained statehood, Israel was invaded by Arab forces enjoying overwhelming superiority in men and weapons. The Hagana, now no longer an outlaw organization but the military arm of a new government, was immediately pressed into service. Sustained by a renewed sense of purpose, the Israeli forces held off the invaders until both sides accepted a one-month United Nations truce on June 11, 1948. During this brief

Infantrymen receiving their basic training

respite, training for large-scale operations was instituted, and the troops learned to use the machines of modern warfare.

Fighting broke out again on July 9, but ten days later the United Nations Security Council imposed a second truce. By that time, the Israelis had cleared some seven hundred square miles of enemy-occupied territory and removed the Arab threat from Tel Aviv, Haifa, and the coastal plain between them. A particularly successful tactic was the use of the familiar jeep, lightly armored, as a speedy and highly mobile offensive weapon.

The second truce ended on October 15, 1948, when Egyptian forces mounted an attack against an Israeli convoy passing near their lines. Now equipped with aircraft, tanks, half-tracks, anti-

Israeli Army signal corpsmen on field maneuvers

aircraft and antitank guns, as well as a small navy, Israel reacted quickly, bombing enemy airfields and armored columns. Early in 1949, the Arab invasion ended in defeat, and armistice agreements were signed between February and July with Egypt, Lebanon, Syria, and Jordan.

With large-scale hostilities ended, the young state was able to give more attention to its economic and social problems. But continuing border incidents and the extension of a technical state of war underscored the need for an effective, battle-ready military establishment.

Israel's leaders decided, in view of the country's elongated shape and miles of exposed border, to have a small, mobile standing army. Efficient and well-motivated, this cadre was equipped to train the thousands of new arrivals to Israel in the use of arms. The "regular army" therefore constitutes a base for total mobilization, when it is necessary.

The Defense Service Law, adopted in 1949, established the framework of military obligation. All men between the ages of eighteen and twenty-six become eligible for twenty-six months of national service. All unmarried women in the same age group are conscripted for twenty months, except for religious girls who do not wish to serve. Deferment is granted to these girls, as it is to a limited number of students.

In developing its defense forces, Israel became the only country in the world to conscript women in peacetime. Girls had fought heroically beside men in the underground armies during the war for independence; it appeared only logical to include them in the military service of the new state. Such conscription also reflects a

Army girls learn the rudiments of machine-gun operation

basic tenet of the young nation—equal status and equal responsibility for women.

Army service for women has another important purpose in
Israel. It helps integrate into the mainstream of the national culture girls from backward countries, giving them a sense of active
participation and imparting to them the basic concepts of democracy. It also helps erase misconceptions about the position of
women among many of the men from Oriental cultures.

In the Israeli Army, women perform essentially administrative
duties to free men for fighting. Some girls serve in the headquar-
ters of infantry battalions. In the main, however, they are clerks,
store-women, telephone operators, instrument checkers, and parachute packers. Others do cultural, welfare, and nursing work.
Official surveys have shown that the presence of women in the
defense forces has an ennobling, beneficial effect on the military.

One of the special problems Israel has had to face in forging
a national army is that presented by the Arab citizens in the country. Service is not compulsory for Arabs, since this might involve
the taking-up of arms against the Arab bands just across the
border. Since 1948, however, numbers of young Moslems, Christians, and Druses have volunteered to serve.

In 1956, at the insistence of the heads of the Druse community, the government finally introduced compulsory military service for the men of this Arabic minority. Druse women have not
been called up, however. A similar request from the Circassians,
another small Moslem group, was subsequently approved, and
their men of military age now serve as well.

Men remain on call in the services until the age of forty-nine;
women without children are reservists until thirty-four. These reserves moved into action almost immediately in the war of 1967

upon the call-up order. Under a territorial organization, each reserve group has its own emergency stores of food and equipment.

Israel's army therefore consists of a regular professional nucleus and the currently serving conscripts and reserves. The Navy and Air Force are composed of volunteers. In overall command of all armed forces is the Chief of the General Staff holding the rank of Rav Aluf, the equivalent of the American major general. Three territorial commanders, as well as the heads of the Navy and Air Force, have the rank of Aluf or brigadier general.

Israeli officials describe their military establishment in terms of defense and the buildup of a strong deterrent force. Much progress in the development of the various corps—infantry, armored, artillery, signal, engineers, parachute, supply, ordnance, and medical—has been made. Increasingly, electronic devices are becoming part of the nation's weaponry.

Young conscript soldiers, both boys and girls, are much in evidence on the streets of Israeli cities and towns. Army vehicles make up much of the traffic on the highways. Army camps laid out in neat company streets are often visible from bus windows to travelers through the countryside. The Army is part of the Israeli experience, and while young servicemen and servicewomen—tanned, lean, and smart-looking in their uniforms—have the universal complaints, their gripes are muted by a realization of the present need for defense and survival.

To insure an adequate supply of officers of all ranks, professional training is provided in military academies. To sustain technical proficiency and fighting spirit—two qualities that have overcome enemy superiority in men and equipment—the government places heavy emphasis on education programs in the armed forces.

New recruits learning Hebrew at an Army camp

Because the nation has given high priority to the absorption of thousands of immigrants, the Army also joins in the training of productive and patriotic citizens. Military service involves the taking of compulsory courses in Hebrew, the Bible, Israeli and general history, geography, mathematics, and civics. These courses are designed to bring every new arrival up to the minimum standard of a basic elementary education.

Military police maintain order, and the Army rabbinate looks after the religious needs of the troops. Recreation and amusement are provided through Army shows, orchestras, and touring theater companies. Welfare problems among the troops are handled by the commanding officers and a Soldiers Welfare Committee, a voluntary public organization. A civil defense network was set up formally in 1951 after the passage of the Civil Defense Act by the Knesset.

Although Israeli defense forces are inexperienced compared with those of other nations, they have extended aid to other young governments in Africa and Latin America through assistance missions. Examples of such military assistance are the paratroop training given to the army of the Congo and the Tanzanian police, the schooling of officers from East African nations, and the establishment of the Ghana Military Flying Academy.

In the conventional military operations of most nations, a considerable percentage of the men under arms are not really "combat effective." For this reason, numerical strength is not always an index of battle efficiency. On the other hand, a small force of determined fighters—like the Biblical Gideon's army—can stand off an opponent though outnumbered ten to one. In 1967, this was demonstrated once again by Israel's defenders, and other young nations have been interested observers.

Yet, along the disputed borders, Israeli soldiers on guard duty —like men on patrol anywhere in the world—"want to go home." They tell an American visitor to the frontier post of the tedium and loneliness as they scan the sloping fields past the enemy positions.

Similarly, all Israelis look forward wistfully to the time when their nation's energies can be turned entirely to the tasks of peace. By tradition, they are a people of the book, rather than the sword. To borrow the lyrics of the popular song from the American musical comedy *Milk and Honey,* "Shalom (peace) is still the nicest word they know."

12 Nahal and Gadna

*I*srael has made two innovations in national defense that have little to do with conventional armies but which may well merit a chapter in the military histories of the future.

First, Israel has found that the people of a disputed territory are the best defense of it. In the past, warring generals would usually clear "a field of fire" and create a "no-man's-land" of such terrain. But in Israel, villages have been built and settled in these frontier zones. The villagers along the border are also its defenders, backed up in depth by similar communities.

Second, Israel has enlisted its youth in the twin tasks of settlement and defense through a kind of semi-militarized domestic peace corps, which antedates by several years its American counterpart. This peace army is made up of two national movements: Gadna, or the youth battalions, and Nahal, or the fighting pioneer youth. Together they form a force which participates in community development projects while retaining a combat capability.

Gadna is a volunteer group of boys and girls, fourteen to eighteen years of age, enlisted from secondary schools, youth organizations, and village settlements. Even before the war for independence, this youth group trained messengers for the Hagana.

Gadna volunteers in training

Later, Gadna volunteers served brilliantly in halting the advance
of a Jordanian legion on Jerusalem. After the war, the group built
a road to Ein Gedi, aided immigrants, took part in archeological
efforts at Masada, and defended settlements against repeated
attacks by the fedayin or Arab infiltrators.

There are about 35,000 young people in Gadna, who regularly attend 120 secondary schools, 35 technical schools, and 21
agricultural schools. Some 10,000 of these members leave their
homes to attend a ten-day military institute each year, taking
specialized courses in air operations, sea service, signaling, and
marksmanship. The boys and girls in Air Gadna learn to pilot light

Gadna officer at Gadna camp

aircraft and gliders and later often qualify as cadets for regular
Air Force training. Naval Gadna offers a course which permits
successful candidates to join the Navy as petty officers.

Gadna training includes work in agricultural camps in the
Negev. In this program, the teen-agers assemble for twenty-one
days at the Gadna farm at Be'er Ora, near Eilat. Here they form
a "garin," or nucleus. The group then stays together until it joins
the Nahal or the regular Army and, at the conclusion of this extended service, often forms a new frontier settlement as a unit.
Israeli experts are assisting in the development of Gadna movements in several countries.

The Nahal is a military-agricultural organization unique among the armies of the world. "Nahal" is an acronym, made up from the initials of Hebrew words meaning "fighting pioneers."

The experiment of Nahal, which is a recognized branch of the Israeli Defense Forces, began in 1949. All members are volunteers who have belonged to the Gadna or other youth movements and who prefer to do their stint of national service in the Nahal instead of the regular Army. They serve for thirty months, of which fewer than twelve are spent in military training. The rest of their tour is devoted to agricultural work on a frontier settlement.

Women in the Nahal take the basic military training plus periodic refresher courses so they may participate in the defense of a settlement. Primarily, they are teachers, social workers, librarians, and agricultural workers.

Nahal girl

A Nahal recruit is a member of a team. When he arrives at his post, he is already part of a garin—a group of boys and girls who have been in the same youth movement and have, in a sense, grown up together. They have shared interests in hobbies, social and cultural activities, leadership of younger children and adolescents, and education programs on domestic and foreign issues.

The young Nahal recruit is trained first to break the soil and to till it effectively, especially in dangerous border areas. He is also trained to handle a gun and to parachute from aircraft in flight.

By induction age, the members of the group have coalesced and have become an entity equipped with a highly developed social

Unit of Nahal girls

consciousness and a sense of association with the aims and values of the young state, attitudes so necessary for cooperative living on the frontier.

An important aspect of the Nahal idea is its use of youth and new immigrants in productive labor. Had they remained tied to their customary urban backgrounds, many of these young people would have been absorbed into service and administrative jobs instead of strengthening the agricultural and construction forces.

The Nahal is now enlarging its programs by sending volunteers on assignments that may not necessarily be agricultural but still important to the nation's development. Some have gone to work as fishermen, and others with special mechanical skills have been given the option of working in factories in new industrial towns. Such work, like other Nahal service, is done in combination with military assignments. One group of Nahal members signed recently for a six-month tour of duty in Dimona, a large development city in the Negev. These Nahal volunteers are teaching, maintaining social services, and participating in municipal government.

At the end of their service, Nahal volunteers are free to do as they please. After the long experience of working together, most remain with the group in the new village they formed, or the infant settlement they helped through difficult days, or the old outpost they aided. Many marry within the garin and continue life in the same unit in which they began their service. The traveler in Israel, if he follows the frontier or ventures into open areas of the country, finds a network of villages—kibbutzim and moshavim—all founded by the Nahal.

In some instances, a Nahal settlement proves to be the magnet that attracts other villages to the same area. The government's project in the desolate Lachish region southwest of Jerusalem is a good example. Three Nahal settlements here along the border provided a buttress for clusters of farmsteads of new immigrants who later settled in the vicinity.

Israel has found that the role of young people in the solution of these problems is crucial, for constructively motivated youth is a powerful force for social and economic progress. On the other hand, if the potential of youth is left undirected, it can become destructive and endanger a nation's stability. In this context, organized movements are of great value, and Israel has been called upon to share its experience with other nations.

The successful union of defense and agricultural and industrial development, as exemplified in the Nahal, has attracted much international attention, particularly among the new nations of Africa. These countries are faced with the problems that adaptation to the demands of the modern state presents to a society based on tribal or local loyalties and traditions.

A youth corps has been established with the aid of Israel in the Ivory Coast, where the *Service Civique* is patterned on the Nahal. A team of Israeli officer-agriculturists work as on-the-spot advisers, teaching the local staff systems of operation. Five training farms have been established, which graduate about a thousand young people every year.

Still another Israeli-guided experiment is the Ivory Coast Women's Project, the first African national service for girls. Its objective is to raise the social status of the African woman and to enable her to develop a partnership with man in the work of nation-building.

In creating new institutions for its own growth and security, Israel has again charted a course for emergent nations throughout the world.

13 Modern Science in an Ancient Land

Israel is the largest producer and exporter of one of the most expensive substances known to man. The country satisfies more than 90 percent of the world's demand for "heavy water," which sells at about a thousand dollars a gram on the international market.

"Heavy water"—really a compound of isotopes—is hardly a popular commodity, although it is important in biological and nuclear research. But for Israel, it is a symbol of the way in which science has been made to serve the economy of the young nation. The manufacture of "heavy water" requires little raw material—mostly brains—and provides tangible evidence that the most valuable natural resources of a country are, after all, the disciplined intelligence and energy of its people.

A scientist turned statesman, President Chaim Weizmann foresaw how Israel would survive despite an unpromising physical environment. "I feel sure that science will bring to this land both peace and a renewal of its youth, creating here the springs of a new material and spiritual life," he once wrote. Nor would pure research be slighted in favor of mere technology. He added: "And here I speak of science for its own sake, and applied science." As

113

Weizmann prophesied, science has enabled a country of two and a half million people, living in what is largely desert, to become economically viable, internationally influential, and militarily defensible.

Scientific research is therefore an important instrument of national policy in Israel, and the National Council for Research and Development, an agency of the Prime Minister's Office, coordinates a variety of activities in this field. Two of its chief affiliates are the National Physical Laboratory and the Negev Institute for Arid Zone Research. Similarly, the Israel Institute for Biological Research is directly attached to the Prime Minister's office.

Much of the work done at these institutions is aimed at increasing the "absorptive capacity" of the nation—its ability to remain open to continued resettlement. This effort includes growing as much food as possible to feed an increased population and cultivating "cash crops" for export.

And so science was first harnessed to agriculture, and scientific farming has been practiced on the land of Israel more intensively than anywhere else in the world. Most cultivators of that parched earth are not born farmers; their lack of experience, however, has proved an advantage as well as a handicap. City dwellers, they are not bound to old ways of tilling the soil. Educated and progressive, they have been eager to apply the findings of scientific research to their labors in the field.

Incidentally, in returning to the soil, many of the early settlers of Israel felt they were renewing an ancient bond. Although the Jews in the ghettos of Europe had been forbidden to own land, many Jewish festivals, such as Succoth (Feast of Tabernacles) and Shavuoth (Pentecost), kept alive a spiritual kinship with

The Feast of the Tabernacles (Succoth)

growing things. Even the old rabbinical writings forbade Jews "to dwell in a town where there are no gardens" and reminded them that "just as others planted for you, so shall you plant for the sake of your children."

In any event, the scientific study of growing things has proved notably successful in Israel. More than five thousand varieties and

Cotton harvest in the Huleh area

species of crops have been imported and tested for adaptability to the arid soil. Citrus fruits were grown almost immediately, and Israeli oranges or "Jaffas" have become the country's chief agricultural export and a mainstay of the economy.

Diversification has followed, and such cash crops as cotton and sugar beets have been developed. Hybrid corn and sorghum were readily adopted from the United States. Even that branch of farming called horticulture has been carefully explored, and Israel now exports cut flowers and bulbs to many parts of the world.

But water is the real key to Israel's agricultural as well as industrial development. Much scientific research is linked to the location of new water resources. About 70 percent of the country's land area—the Negev—is desert; this region must be made to flower if the absorptive capacity of the nation is to be expanded.

Israel's efforts to tap new sources of water have implications for the vast arid regions of the Arab East as well. In a speech before an American audience, U.S. Secretary of the Interior Stewart L. Udall urged Israel's Arab neighbors to follow that nation's "wonderful example of land reclamation and development," pointing out that even now, "in a hostile climate, Israel had created a living and life-supporting environment."

Israeli hydrological research has also aroused considerable interest in the United States, where periodic local water shortages have become a matter of national concern. In fact, on a planet whose population seems to be multiplying more rapidly than its resources, it is not too much to say that Israel has become a laboratory for all mankind.

As long ago as the Biblical Exodus, water seems to have been a problem. The Old Testament account tells how Moses struck a rock with his staff, and water came forth for the thirsty Israelites. But the water was brackish—as it still is in much of the country—and only after Moses sweetened it with a tree divinely revealed to him, could it be drunk. Modern scientific research must repeat the miracle.

Related to the work in hydrology is the research in oceanography and marine biology conducted at the new Israeli Marine Laboratory at Eilat. A $220,000 facility, the scientific center has studied three hundred different species of fish.

A visitor to Israel is struck by the absence of the rivers and streams so familiar to the American landscape. Even the storied Jordan River is, by American standards, really no more than a creek. Yet intensive exploitation of these meager sources is an important aspect of the water development program.

Jordan River in Upper Galilee

A network of wells has been drilled throughout the land, often to a depth of thousands of feet. In charting the movement of underground streams, Israeli geologists and physicists have teamed up; with radioactive isotopes, water has been "labeled" and traced. Even deep below the surface of the Negev Desert, water has been located by the use of these new scientific techniques.

One of the most interesting experiments has involved going back two thousand years to the methods used by the ancient Nabateans, an enterprising desert people, in farming the Negev. Modern hydrologists, or water scientists, have discovered that the Nabateans trapped rainwater through an intricate pattern of "runoff" planting. Experimental farms were built at Mamshis, Avdat, and Shivta just as they might have been in the days of antiquity, along with new measuring devices. Many varieties of trees and vegetables are now grown in the desert soil by imitating a long-vanished civilization.

The experimental farm near Avdat brought in a bumper crop of asparagus, and there was successful cultivation of peaches, apricots, almonds, and loganberries. Plans are under way to extend the principle used—individual catchment basins or water-collecting areas for each fruit tree rather than basins for groves or larger sections. Two desert kibbutzim—Revivim and Mashabei Sadeh, settlements located between Avdat and Beersheba—are among the important centers for such experimentation.

If the Israelis could realize an ancient dream and learn to sweeten or "desalinate" salt water, the problem would be resolved. Pioneering experiments in desalination are being conducted along various lines. Research utilizing a procedure called electrodialysis is being done at the Negev Institute for Arid Zone Research in Beersheba. By this process an electric current is passed through special membranes—thin sheets of organic tissue acting as filters—to separate the salt from the water. A pilot unit in the desert using electrodialysis is already producing 125,000 gallons a day.

Another promising method of desalination is the Zarchin process, based on the principle of freezing sea water to remove the salt. A model working plant has been erected on the Gulf of Aqaba to freeze the tropical waters of the Red Sea.

But a third way of sweetening salt water promises the most for the future. It utilizes atomic energy to produce electric power as well as fresh water in the conversion process. This method of desalination was the basis of a 1964 agreement between President Lyndon Johnson and Prime Minister Levi Eshkol to set up a joint American-Israeli project.

The atomic-energy powered plant envisioned under this U.S.—Israeli agreement will supply two hundred megawatts of electricity and over a hundred million cubic meters of fresh water each year. It should be in operation by 1970, and its success may well determine the course of history. With water, the vast reaches of the Sahara—of Arabia Deserta—could conceivably support a population of millions.

On another front, much scientific research in Israel, as in the United States, has been directed at the elimination of disease. Along with other countries of the East, the people of Israel once had a low life-expectancy and a high infant-mortality rate. Tropical diseases, such as malaria, bilharzia, and trachoma, exacted a heavy toll. The largely unrestricted immigration of people from all over the world—many of them survivors of disease-ridden concentration camps—and their crowding into temporary reception centers presented an additional threat of epidemic.

But today, the life-expectancy and the infant-mortality rates

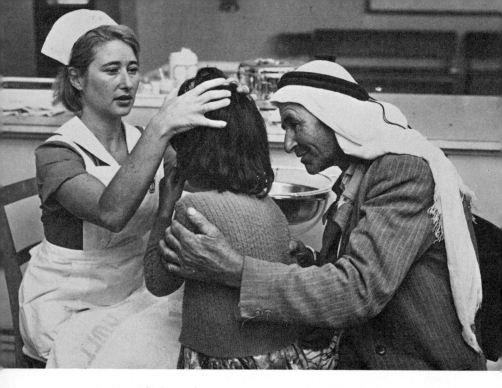

Arab child getting treatment at health clinic near Haifa

in Israel are on a par with those in the most advanced nations of
the West. Preventive medicine, epidemiology, and public health
are important areas of government concern. The population of
Israel, by far the healthiest in the Near East, again serves as an
experimental group for other Afro-Asian nations. An Israeli medical team, for example, has been engaged with a hospital in Ran-
goon, Burma, in a joint research project in endemic anemias.

A curious facet of the public health program overlaps the
sciences of anthropology and sociology. The Jews who have im-
migrated to Israel do not have any distinctive "Jewish" appearance; in height, complexion, color of eyes and hair, they resemble
the nationals of the countries they come from. They understand-

ably prefer the customs and foods of those peoples. Israel, therefore, provides a unique laboratory for studying how heredity, diet, and folkways affect physical and mental health.

For example, why do the Jews from Oriental countries suffer less from diabetes and heart disease than those from Europe? Why do the immigrants from Africa rarely have tooth decay? And why are those desert nomads, the Bedouins, almost free from athero- sclerosis—one of the main causes of death in the United States? These questions have claimed the attention of the American Na- tional Institute of Health, and a U.S.–Israel team is now involved in a long-term research project.

In still another field of investigation, higher mathematics— often regarded as a "pure" science—has served a number of prac- tical purposes in Israel. Working with geologists, members of the applied mathematics department of the Weizmann Institute joined in a successful search for oil resources. A formula for predicting tides has also been evolved, and a great earthquake in Chile was mathematically foreseen by scientists at the Institute. Incidentally, the new computer constructed there is called the Golem, named for the legendary automaton said to have been created by Rabbi Judah Loew of Prague during the Middle Ages.

With no waterpower and limited fuel resources, Israel has given high priority to the scientific development of new sources of energy. For tropical countries—indeed for a world in which stores of such fossil fuels as oil and coal are being rapidly depleted—the collection and storage of solar heat would be a tremendous ad- vance. Israeli scientists recently invented a generator powered by sunshine to produce electricity, and solar heaters for domestic use are already manufactured commercially.

Similarly, much experimentation is directed at the exploitation of atomic energy. The first atomic reactor in Israel, of the "swimming pool" type, was completed at Nahal Sorek in 1960, and several others are now under construction, including a major installation at Dimona. As in the United States, there is an Atomic Energy Commission in charge of such research.

In all of these areas of inquiry, Israel sees science primarily in terms of national survival. But the government and the people also understand that knowledge can have no boundaries, as the many joint projects with foreign scientists attest. All of mankind is certain to share the benefits of new discoveries from the ancient land.

14 Digging Up the Past

Israel is literally a treasure house for the archeologist. From all over the world, scientists have come to the storied land to probe gently beneath the dust of centuries for buried cities, as well as for bone fragments, crude tools, and bits of flint and rock art. James Michener's best-selling novel, *The Source,* presented in fictionalized form an account of one such expedition.

Thoroughly aware of its importance in archeological research, Israel has begun an intensive mapping survey of the entire country, which may take from ten to fifteen years. Under the auspices of the government's Department of Antiquities and the Israel Museum, ten teams of five men each are taking part in the study. One team has begun work in the northern area around the ancient seaport of Atlit near Haifa, where it has photographed and mapped 178 sites, of which only about 60 were known previously. A second team has started work in the south, near Sdeh Boker in the Negev.

Israeli youth are deeply involved in this archeological activity. Young people have a consciousness of the buried past as a significant element in their country's cultural life and as a valuable resource. In addition, archeology is almost a national pastime; the opportunity to participate in a "dig" stimulates as much excitement among Israeli youth as the World Series does among young Americans. And rare is the visitor to Israel who does not search excavation sites successfully for coins or bits of glass and pottery of an earlier time.

Much of the research has confirmed the historical basis of Biblical accounts. As the instigator of archeological efforts and as a seat of scholarship in the science, the young nation has again exerted an influence disproportionate to its size and population.

But Israel's interest in the past is more than an expression of nascent nationalism or a desire to test the Scriptures. Although religious and ethnic pride are always present, the young nation is turning increasingly to archeology for help in understanding why some societies succeed and others fail and whether patterns of ancient life can provide clues to survival in the open desert.

Along with its neighbors on the Mediterranean coast—Egypt, Greece, Italy, and others—Israel has had such intensive ancient occupation that it is difficult not to find remains of one period or another almost anywhere beneath its surface. Open digs or excavations revealing striking examples of ancient architecture, and "tels," or artificial hills covering ancient sites, mark the countryside.

So important a facet of Israeli life is archeological research that the government has taken over the job of safeguarding the ancient places through its Department of Antiquities in the Ministry of Education and Culture. The department is responsible for enforcing the Antiquities Law, which controls all excavations through a system of government licensing.

The department has also been able to enlist amateurs throughout the country to participate on a regional basis in the watching and recording of relics and in the development of local and rural museums. Typical of these museum collections are the exhibits at

Hazorea, Revivim, Ma'ayam, Baruch, Sedot Yam, Ein Harod, and Shar Hagolan. New municipal museums have been opened in Haifa, Tel Aviv, Beersheba, Netanya, and Tiberias.

Two archeological events—the expedition to Masada and the discovery of the Dead Sea Scrolls—have become landmarks of modern science. Masada—the windswept rock in the Judean desert where Herod built his palace-fortress and where the Hebrews made their last desperate stand against the might of Rome—occupies a special place in the mind and heart of Israel. Archeologists agree on Masada's vast scientific significance, but, in addition, it has captured the imagination of the world as a symbol of courage and as a monument to the ancestral hero figures of Israel. It has become a shrine for the youth of the new nation, and thousands of them flock there regularly to pay homage to their forebears who chose death rather than Roman captivity.

Masada stands at the eastern edge of the desert, towering some thirteen hundred feet above the Dead Sea about twenty dusty, curving miles north of Sodom. There is little life here, and the rocky landscape has a savage beauty. The fortress is part of the stark pattern of browns, buffs, and whites, unyielding except to wind and weather which carve strange, random figures out of the rough formations.

What is known of Masada comes largely from the record left by the Jewish historian Josephus Flavius, a military officer in the Galilee who went over to the Romans. The elaborate fortifications, siege works, and palaces were built by Herod between 36 and 30 B.C. Subsequently, Roman soldiers were garrisoned there, until 66 A.D., when a group of Jewish zealots led by Menahem captured the fortress and wiped out the Roman legionnaires. The Jewish forces were joined by refugees from Jerusalem after its fall in 70 A.D.

Using Masada as their base, the Jews raided Roman encampments so frequently and successfully that in 72 A.D., Flavius Silva, the Roman governor, vowed to crush this outpost of resistance. He marched on Masada with an army of about six thousand, establishing a camp at the base of the rock. Far above, Eleazar ben Yair, the commander, prepared for the defense, using both the natural and man-made fortifications.

In April of the following year, the Romans completed construction of a ramp along the western side of Masada, erected a siege tower, and moved a battering ram up the ramp to breach the fortress. Aided by favorable winds, they tossed over lighted torches, igniting the wooden casemate wall to insure an easy entry on the following day.

Eleazar ben Yair knew that the struggle was ended and that

A section of Herod's Palace at Masada

only a few hours remained before the superior Roman force would move in. There were only two choices: surrender or death. As Josephus recorded the episode, Eleazar decided on "a death of glory" in preference to "a life of infamy."

The defenders—960 men, women, and children—ended their lives by their own hands. When the Romans gained the summit the next morning, they were met by a sight that stunned them. Josephus, in his description, wrote:

> And so met (the Romans) with the multitude of the slain, but could take no pleasure in the fact, though it were done to their enemies. Nor could they do other than wonder at the courage of their resolution, and at the immovable contempt of death which so great a number of them had shown when they went through with such an action as that was.

The excavations at Masada were conducted over two seasons —from October, 1963, to May, 1964, and from November, 1964, to April, 1965—by an expedition led by Yigael Yadin. Some two thousand volunteers from Israel and twenty-eight foreign countries participated eagerly in the dig. Israeli youth were particularly industrious, of course, and young kibbutzniks—workers from the agricultural settlements—strove with new pride to reconstruct the relics of the heroic defenders of the fortress.

Unlike many other archeological expeditions, in which finds are often accidental, the Masada excavation was the result of long-range planning, military discipline, and dedicated effort by volunteers as well as professional scientists. The hazards that are part of any major dig were increased by exceptionally severe winter weather, sixty-mile-an-hour winds, and cloudbursts that washed out access roads. There were times when the party could be supplied only by helicopter.

Archeologists' camp overlooking the Dead Sea at Masada

The cloudbursts—inconvenient though they were—incidentally served an important function. They demonstrated to Professor Yadin and his staff how ingeniously Herod provided for a water supply through an elaborate multi-level system of conduits and cisterns.

As the professional and amateur archeologists began their probing—slowly, gently, gingerly—the relics of a people and a civilization came out of the dust. Pieces of buildings, frescoes, skeletons, food, coins, armor, religious articles, pottery, tools, utensils—each item was marked, catalogued, and brought carefully down from the mountain for study and reassembly.

Soon the plan of Masada began to unfold. Here were palaces, storerooms, a synagogue, apartments, the zealots' living quarters, a ritual bath, a swimming pool, a throne room, a water gate, and other evidences of life nineteen hundred years ago.

Youthful diggers turned up some remarkable literary finds— Chapters 18 through 85 of the Book of Psalms and a fragment from Chapters 8 through 11 of Leviticus, describing some of the dietary laws to which observant Jews still adhere today. A young girl worker found a fragment of writing in small, clear Hebrew script, which turned out to be Psalm 150—the last chapter.

One of the most significant religious items established a link between Qumran, the site of the discovery of the Dead Sea Scrolls in 1947, and Masada. It is a fragment of Sabbath liturgy based on a Qumran calendar identical with the text of a Dead Sea Scroll. Another spectacular literary discovery was a first-century B.C. copy of part of the lost Hebrew original of Ecclesiasticus, the apocryphal wisdom book of Ben Sira, which before this time had been known only in the Greek, Syriac, and Latin versions.

The discovery of the Dead Sea Scrolls and the cloak-and-dagger story of their return to Israel constitute another fantastic archeological adventure. The precious manuscripts were first found in a cave in the Jordanian section of Palestine, just as the United Nations was terminating the British mandate. Seven years elapsed, however, between the discovery of the scrolls by some passing Bedouins and their acquisition for Hebrew University.

The late Professor E. L. Sukenik has been credited with first appreciating the tremendous importance of the discovery, and he and his son, Yigael Yadin of subsequent Masada fame, gained possession of three of the scrolls. But four others could not be obtained, and the scientists despaired of ever assuring the preservation of the priceless manuscripts.

Then, a year after Professor Sukenik's death in 1953, Yadin

Yigael Yadin, former
Chief of Staff of the
Israel Army, at a
garden party, con-
versing with General
Riley, former Chief
U.N. Observer

was in the United States on a lecture tour. He discovered through a newspaper advertisement that, inexplicably, the remaining scrolls were for sale! After answering the advertisement, he embarked upon delicate negotiations with an agent of the Syrian Orthodox Church. A sale price of $250,000 was finally set, and the scrolls were promptly bought. On the morning of July 2, 1954, a large black trunk containing the precious manuscripts was on its way from the Waldorf-Astoria Hotel in New York City to the Israeli consulate.

News of the acquisition was made public by Prime Minister Sharett only on February 13, 1955. At that time, it was also re- vealed that the purchase was made possible through the generosity of the late D. Samuel Gottesman, a New York industrialist.

Originally preserved in sealed clay jars, the scrolls are evidently the remnants of the library of a pre-Christian monastic sect, the Essenes. Probably annihilated by the Romans in about 100 A.D., the Essenes left cached in the caves a nearly complete copy of

Isaiah and fragments of other Biblical writings which antedate manuscripts previously known. The scrolls also contain the *Manual of Discipline* of the communal sect, whose practices and thinking were influential in determining the direction of early Christianity.

Today, the scrolls are housed in an exciting-looking building called The Shrine of the Book in Jerusalem, near the Israel Museum complex. The structure, designed by architects Frederick J. Kiesler and Armand P. Bartos, is of black basalt with a towering white dome. Entrance is through a tunnel formed by a series of trapezoid-shaped arches. The interior design conveys to the visitor the story of the scrolls and a description of the cave in which they were found. Constant temperature and humidity controls are maintained for the preservation of the documents, which have had an incalculable impact on theological and historical scholarship.

The finds at Qumran and Masada stimulated additional efforts to roll back the limits of knowledge of mankind's beginnings at the sites of one of the earliest civilizations. And these diggings have in turn led to other expeditions, other adventures, other epochal discoveries.

Shrine of the Book, which houses the Dead Sea Scrolls

15 *Still Beneath the Surface*

But science is more than a few isolated dramatic discoveries. In addition to the startling illuminations of the past found at Masada and Qumran, painstaking archeological research almost daily brings new secrets out of the soil of Israel. All have become part of the cumulative store of man's knowledge.

It is noteworthy that the young nation, despite the host of problems directly linked to its very survival, has stubbornly refused to permit the archeological effort to flag. Investing manpower and capital, the new state has given high priority to the excavation of historic sites—at least partially because of the need to redevelop and populate these areas in the near future. It is hoped that everything of scientific importance will have been uncovered before the bulldozers work over the land, obliterating many of its features forever.

Intensive diggings began soon after independence was attained. Israeli and French archeologists launched a cooperative project on Palestine's Neolithic civilization (c. 6000 B.C.) as well as the Chalcolithic period (c. 4500-3200 B.C.). In 1961, a Japanese scientific mission probed Israel's prehistory and found, in a cave at Nahal

Amud in the Upper Galilee, the skeleton of a Neanderthal man of the Pleistocene Age, perhaps 500,000 years old.

Other scientific work has been done and continues to be done on sites dating back to the early Bronze Age (c. 3000-2100 B.C.), when the Canaanites occupied the land. Their earliest city civilization was found at Beit Yerah on the southwest shore of the Sea of Galilee.

Of special interest to archeologists studying the Middle Bronze Age that came some six hundred years later have been the four seasons of excavations conducted by the James A. De Rothschild Expedition at Hazor, in the northeastern corner of the Galilee, under the auspices of the Hebrew University, the Anglo-Israel Exploration Society, and the Israeli government. Made famous by the Book of Joshua, Hazor was the capital of the northern Canaanite kingdoms. Evidence found here suggests that the city was captured and burned by the Israelites in the thirteenth century B.C., just as the Bible relates.

In the late Bronze Age (c. 1500-1200 B.C.), archeological evidence reveals that Egyptians ruled Palestine. Their power declined in time under the impact of a series of invasions, including that of the Hebrews. Excavations in 1955-58 on the site of ancient Jaffa, just north of Tel Aviv, uncovered the walls of a citadel and gate erected by Ramses II of Egypt.

Digs at Tel Kassile on the northern edge of Tel Aviv, at Ramat Rachel south of Jerusalem, and additional research at Megiddo—the Biblical Armageddon—southeast of Haifa, have provided new insights into the royal period of Israel and Judah during the Iron Age, 1200-900 B.C. In many of these expeditions, American scientists and young people were active and enthusiastic participants.

Archeological surveys in the Negev have shown that the ancient kings of Judah extended their influence and control southward as far as Sinai, even after the reign of Solomon. It is now known that in the period of the United Kingdom (tenth century B.C.), Jewish settlement and agriculture spread well into the central Negev.

The discovery of the scrolls near the Dead Sea and the exploration of Masada in the same general area have led to continued surveys in that section of the country for other materials. In 1960-61, archeologists made a major find at Nahal Hever, some sixty miles north of Masada in the general vicinity of Ein Gedi. Here, just south of the Jordanian border on the western shore of the Dead Sea, diggers found the caves in which Shimon Bar

Archeologists examine finds in the Judean Desert

Caves where the Bar Kochba letters were found

Kochba and his followers took refuge after the last revolt against
Roman rule in 132-35 A.D.

The Army joined hundreds of volunteers, scientists, university
students, members of kibbutzim and moshavim, and young people
from the cities and from abroad in exploring the caves in a gorge
leading down to the sea. Here, too, the finds were both historical
and literary, bringing to life again a legendary figure whose warrior
band embraced a Masada-like death.

Found in the caves, along with combs, sandals, ceremonial
objects, mirrors, glass plates, cooking pots, and other household
equipment, was a bundle of papyri containing fifteen letters from

Bar Kochba in Hebrew, Aramaic, and Greek. Later, the expedition found a second bundle of documents relating to Bar Kochba's
daughter and giving intimate details of life at the time. Taken together, this evidence confirmed Roman accounts and the Jewish
traditional version of the Bar Kochba revolt.

Jewish history of the Talmudic period has also been illumi-
nated by excavations at Beit She'arim, at the western end of the
Plains of Esdraelon. Here is the site of a small town, known to
have been built in the Israelite period, which became (about 200
A.D.) the home of the Patriarch Judah the Prince, first editor of
the Mishnah, an interpretation of Biblical law.

Another major excavation site showing Roman influence is

**Remains of the triple arch at the entrance to the tomb of
Judah the Prince, editor of the "Mishnah," 2nd century**

Harbor fortifications at Caesarea

located at Caesarea on the Mediterranean coast. Here, at Herod's
city, the capital of the ancient Roman province of Judea, are
waterworks, harbor installations, and the famous outdoor
theater.

The theater was unearthed in 1959-61 by an Italian expedition. Archeologists at that time found a fragmentary inscription
bearing the name of Pontius Pilate. This is considered the first
epigraphical evidence of that Biblical personality's historical existence. At Caesarea, visitors are given an opportunity to engage in
amateur archeology. A search through the ruins or at the theater
usually turns up a souvenir of an earlier age.

Roman aqueduct leading from Carmel range to Caesarea

Another Roman theater was recently uncovered at Beit She'an on Israel's eastern border, south of the Sea of Galilee.

Not only have Israelis opened their land and given technical and financial aid to foreign expeditions, but they have given the science of archeology an important tool—the method of stratigraphical digging. This is a technique by which archeologists can peel away strata from the top down.

For the Israeli, archeology has proved a direct link with the past and has given him roots after a lifetime of dispersion and wandering. For the Jew of the Diaspora, it has provided a continuity with his forebears and a sense of having a spiritual homeland which is nevertheless based on historical reality.

16 The National Economy

*A*lthough located geographically so that it is a link to three continents, Israel is at the same time—paradoxically—unable to exploit this advantage because of that very geographical situation and the concomitant political problems. It is surrounded by the sea and hostile neighbors, has poor natural resources, a severely limited supply of water, and few sources of energy.

There is some mineral wealth in deposits of potash, bromides, and magnesium in the Dead Sea, phosphate in the Negev, and copper ore in the southern reaches of the country. And yet, on this unsteady base, the young nation has built a viable, expanding economic structure, which is supporting a growing population.

Such rapid expansion under difficult conditions has often been contrary to accepted traditional economic concepts, but, at the same time, some of the dramatic and unorthodox approaches have provided a guide for other nations just emerging from colonialism.

The topography and climate of Israel are surprisingly varied for a country of its size. Visitors unused to days on end of sunny, cloudless skies sometimes complain of the perfect weather. Pleasant and healthful, the climate is hot in the summer, reminding the American tourist of Florida. However, it is often brisk and cool in the hills of Jerusalem—particularly in the evenings—growing increasingly warmer as one travels farther south.

The rains come between November and April, the Israeli winter—some thirty inches in the north and only about two inches in the south. The most uncomfortable weather is brought by the "hamseen," a hot, dry wind from the desert regions of Jordan. Derived from the Arabic word for "fifty," the hamseen is supposed to come for fifty days a year, in May and October. The Hebraic equivalent for this climatic phenomenon is *"sharav."*

Topographically, the landscape changes markedly as a traveler proceeds from north to south. In the north, the fertile hill country of the Galilee and the rolling hills around Jerusalem slope down to flat plains that follow the gentle westward curve of the Mediterranean coast. Along the eastern border runs the deep valley of the

The dry, empty central Negev

Jordan River. But the southern half of the country is almost entirely the dry, empty Negev, which narrows sharply to a six-mile base at Eilat on the Red Sea.

Since statehood, the nation's economy has been essentially agricultural, but in recent years there has been a decided increase in industrial production. In this connection, again, Israel's great asset has been its people. The growth of the population and the special character of each wave of immigration have helped determine the economic course of the young country.

Several parallels from the history of other nations come to mind. The Puritans brought their skills to America, the country of their adoption, as did the Huguenot refugees from France in the days of the Reformation. Flemish weavers developed the wool industry in England, and the Russian Jewish immigrants of the 1890's promoted the manufacture of clothing in the United States. Traditionally and naturally, artisans and craftsmen seek to pursue their old occupations under new conditions.

The new immigrants to Israel gave their country a pool of hard-working skilled labor, a reservoir of managerial talent, and a supply of professional and technical workers, all available at low wages by American standards. They also constituted a large domestic market and, with imported capital, provided the ingredients for further industrialization of the basically agricultural nation.

Since statehood, industrial output has risen tenfold, and the export of goods has increased fourteenfold to a figure in excess of $406,000,000. In recent years, exports rose to 50 percent of imports, as against 11–12 percent in 1949. The number of vessels in shipping went from four in 1948 to ninety in 1965, and tonnage rose from 6,000 in 1948 to 932,000 in 1965. Agricultural increases were just as dramatic.

The high-speed economy ran into its first major roadblock in 1965-66. In 1965, immigration fell off and continued to drop in the following year. A cutback in housing and in some public works projects produced a sudden unemployment problem in a land that had previously suffered from *over*employment or a labor shortage. Together with the trade deficit—that is, more imports than exports—the economy was strained sufficiently to compel the government to formulate a plan for economic reform.

The plan imposed restraints in wages, prices, and taxes to ease the trade gap—the excess of imports over exports—and unemployment, phenomena which the government maintained were interrelated. It also funneled surplus manpower into export industries and directed that a higher proportion of capital investment go into these industries.

After four months, the government admitted that the economic reform plan had been too extreme—in fact, unemployment increased threefold during 1966—but announced that it would stay with the plan as a weapon against Israel's first major recession.

Although the pace of the economy was slowed, the nation continued to make some significant gains, particularly in increasing its exports and thereby narrowing the trade gap. Industrial growth was maintained with the development of an automobile industry, the building of oil refineries in the north and at Eilat—the rapidly developing port city on the Red Sea—and the increased activity in diamonds, ceramics, textiles, minerals, and aeronautics.

Agriculture is remarkably successful in Israel, and the output per acre is among the highest in the world. Water continues to be a limiting factor, but constant research into new techniques of irrigation, water collection, and desalination holds great promise.

Citrus exports increase annually as the Israelis develop special growing techniques to speed ripening. The use of vast fields of plastic covers to step up the maturing process has given Israeli oranges the advantage of getting to European markets weeks before the competing produce of Spain and Italy.

Tourism, actively promoted by the government, has become a major industry in Israel. Recognition of this development warranted the recent conversion of the Government Tourist Corporation into a Ministry of Tourism. Plans are being made to bring six hundred thousand tourists to Israel annually in the next few years.

Construction is under way of facilities for Christian pilgrims who come in increasing numbers to visit the holy places of Jerusalem and Nazareth. New tourist accommodations are also being erected near the hot-water springs of Tiberias and the baths at Ein Bokek on the Dead Sea.

While the Israeli government, in its broad general design, tends toward the welfare state, the economy is mixed. It includes private, state-owned, and cooperative enterprises. Most plants in the country—about 65 percent of the total industrial investment—are privately owned. State undertakings account for some 20 percent; most of these are devoted to the exploitation of natural resources in the Negev, projects involving risks which private capital is rarely willing to assume. The remainder—about 15 percent—consists of enterprises run by cooperatives, or companies controlled by Histadrut, the General Federation of Labor. In some industries, there is a combination of two or three forms of ownership in competitive coexistence. There are also some thirty thousand shops and small factories, operated by sixty thousand persons.

But statistics are rather dull. The significant story behind the figures is that sustained economic growth at an accelerated pace can be achieved in a democratic regime provided there is a contin-

Experimental farm in the Negev

uous infusion of capital and labor—money and people. There is one other condition: the people must be energetic, cooperative, and industrious.

Israel's most pressing economic problem has been, and continues to be, inflation. This condition is partially related to the nation's adverse trade balance. Some progress has been made in attaining a more favorable ratio of wealth flowing in and out of the country, even though unpopular policies have had to be invoked. Incidentally, the Israeli pound is pegged to the American dollar, and the persistent effort is to maintain a relative value of three pounds to a dollar.

The standard of living in Israel is quite high and compares

Window displays
at John Wanamaker,
Philadelphia,
during Israel Week

with that of other advanced nations of the world. Recent statistics show that, of every ten families in Israel, five own electric refrigerators, nine own radio sets, and seven have gas ranges. While this may not approach American standards, it is on a level with averages in several European countries. Israel's per capita income in 1965 was $1,069, compared with $1,439 in Great Britain, $1,379 in France, $1,368 in Belgium, and $885 in Italy.

While the government still seeks to hew closely to its original welfare-state ideal, subtle changes have been taking place in the Israeli economy. The fairly equal distribution of income among the population, characteristic of the state in its early years, has been altered in the last decade. The accumulation of wealth in some sectors as a result of technological changes, inflation, and a rise in land values has been noted. The arrival of immigrant groups with lower levels of education and skill has contributed toward this trend. In the newly established development towns populated mainly by immigrants, standards of living are lower than in the older settlements, but efforts continue to narrow the difference.

Israel has covered its foreign currency deficit from various outside sources, but obviously the young nation must reduce its dependence on foreign aid and become more self-sufficient if it is to achieve stable and lasting economic health. Toward this end, private organizations and government agencies have tried to boost exports through foreign trade fairs, including some in relatively new markets. Israel has been represented in as many as thirty-five exhibitions in recent years in many countries. Goods made in Israel are also being promoted through "Israel Weeks" in department stores throughout the world.

The Foreign Trade Division in the Ministry of Commerce and Industry has introduced a series of export incentives to encourage manufacturers. Among the incentives offered have been reductions in dock and bank charges, export risk insurance, and increases in exporters' credits. Leading exporters may also earn "prestige" honors. Firms that exported more than a million dollars' worth of goods were recently honored by the President of Israel at his official residence in Jerusalem on "Export Day."

This silent war for economic existence continues day by day on many fronts. Not so dramatic, perhaps, as the military battles for national independence, it is nevertheless an important aspect of the grim struggle for survival in today's world.

17 *Israel on the World Stage*

In a world dominated by two or three great powers, life can be difficult for a small nation. Many of the emergent states of Africa and Asia have therefore chosen, as their pattern for survival, alignment with one or another of the major political blocs. On the other hand, a few fortunate young nations—geographically remote from the centers of international rivalry—have been able to develop in statehood without direct involvement in the power struggles of our time.

In taking her place in the world community, Israel has sought to follow an independent foreign policy, avoiding commitment to any military-defense system such as NATO, SEATO, or the Warsaw Pact. At the same time—as has been true throughout history—the facts of geography have precluded a policy of isolation. Instead, the tiny country has had thrust upon it almost overwhelming diplomatic and military tasks.

Ushered into statehood by one of the earliest important actions of the United Nations, Israel fully understands the interdependence of peoples in today's world. A member of the UN since May, 1949, she enjoyed, until 1967, diplomatic and consular relations with nearly every nation outside the Arab League, maintaining

Abba Eban leading the Israeli delegation at an
international conclave

missions in eighty-five countries on every continent. Common
cultural traditions and dedication to democratic institutions have
made her ties with the Western World particularly close.

Israeli foreign policy has been almost desperately directed at
the achievement of a lasting peace—both in the Near East and
in the world at large—so that the work of reclaiming the ancient
land and integrating a polyethnic society might go forward without diversion. In addition, the urgent tasks of industrialization and
the struggle for economic independence have had irresistible claims
on the energies and resources of the young nation. For these reasons, Israel has repeatedly proclaimed strong support for the
principles of the UN Charter, particularly those providing for
amicable settlement of international differences.

In seeking to strengthen the UN, Israel has recommended
changes in the structure of the organization to reflect altered relationships between nations. For example, Israel favors the enlarge-
ment of the Security Council and the Economic and Social Council
to include some of the newly independent nations. She also has

(Above): David Ben-Gurion welcomes African visitors;
(Below): Israeli agricultural expert confers with African
community leaders on improving farming methods

called for "universality of membership"—the inclusion of states now barred from representation in the international body.

A long-time sufferer under alien rule, Israel has further subscribed to the principle that no nation should dominate another. She has given support, in and out of the UN, to peoples under colonial rule aspiring toward independence. Free from the imperialistic taint and racial biases of other advanced nations, Israel has also been in a particularly strategic position to offer—and have accepted—technical and economic assistance to the countries of Asia and Africa.

The relationship between Israel and the United States has always been a special one, and it deserves closer examination in even a brief analysis of Israeli foreign affairs. Officially, the United States has regarded the young nation with a mixture of affection, admiration, and occasional annoyance. The American people are overwhelmingly pro-Israel in sentiment, as public opinion polls demonstrated during the 1967 crisis.

President Harry S. Truman was a staunch advocate of Israeli independence, and statehood was achieved in 1948 with the support of his administration. In 1952, a United States Operations Missions Office was opened in Israel to coordinate the various forms of American technical aid to the young nation. Within ten years, however, its job was completed, both cooperating governments agreeing that Israel had progressed sufficiently to warrant closing out the program.

President John F. Kennedy holds a unique place in the affections of the young nation. An impressive Kennedy Memorial located near Jerusalem was dedicated on July 4, 1966, in the presence of a distinguished American delegation headed by Chief Justice Earl Warren. This shrine to the martyred President con-

Kennedy Memorial Monument before completion

sists of a circular building of modern design on an elliptical plaza of dark granite. A small museum houses a collection of documents and pictures dealing with Israel-American relations. Each of fifty-one windows bears the emblem of a state of the union (and the District of Columbia) while in the center burns an eternal flame.

Interior of Kennedy Memorial Monument

The memorial overlooks the Kennedy Peace Forest, a reclamation project clothing formerly bare, eroded hills with five million trees.

President Lyndon B. Johnson's administration was deeply concerned in the events of 1967. In the Security Council, the United States at first sought vainly to keep the peace; after war broke out, America helped to arrange the cease-fire. Later, in the emergency General Assembly session called by the Soviet Union, the United States successfully opposed an Arab-Soviet bloc resolution directed against Israel.

President Johnson took issue with Egypt's critical decision to blockade the Gulf of Aqaba, a move that led to the fury of all-out war. But after the cease-fire, he questioned the Israeli annexation of the Old City of Jerusalem formerly occupied by Jordan, advocating instead internationalization of the ancient quarter.

Investment in Israel—as exemplified in the Tel Aviv-Hilton Hotel, the Ford assembly plant, and Coca-Cola—has attracted American capital. Nearly a billion dollars' worth of State of Israel Bonds have been sold in America. Aside from the philanthropy of Americans of Jewish faith, many non-Jews have been generous contributors to Israeli cultural institutions. Such a popular personality as Frank Sinatra, for example, financed the construction of a youth center in Nazareth.

As has been observed, day-to-day developments in world diplomacy do not always find even the closest international friends acting in concert or with consistency. In September, 1962, America agreed to supply the Israeli Defense Forces with Hawk ground-to-air missiles, but in January, 1967, the United States gave jet planes to Jordan, a nation at war with Israel. In September, 1963, the United States could condemn Syrian aggression at Almagor, while censuring a retaliatory Israeli raid on the Jordanian village of Es

Samu in December, 1966. As an ironic commentary on our times, when war broke out in 1967, Israel's American-made tanks were locked in combat with Jordan's American-made tanks.

A particularly unfortunate episode in Israeli–U.S. relations was the attack on an American ship by Israel's naval and air forces during the 1967 war. Both nations agreed that the attack was accidental, and apologies and compensation were immediately offered. But the incident served to illustrate the difficulties that will arise in times of crisis between nations that have an essential community of interest.

America's cold-war rival, the Soviet Union, supported statehood for Israel in the United Nations in 1948, but has been increasingly unfriendly in recent years as the new nation took an independent line in world affairs. The U.S.S.R. vetoed the pro-Israel resolution on Almagor in the UN Security Council; nevertheless, Israel endorsed the Soviet Premier's note on the peaceful settlement of international disputes just three months later. In 1967, the Soviet Union armed Egypt and Syria and strongly supported the Arab war effort.

Relations between Israel and the Soviet Union—as well as the Soviet-bloc nations—have been periodically troubled by disagreements involving the migration of Jews from Eastern Europe. From time to time, the Communist nations have relaxed restrictions on migration, but then closed their borders to those seeking to leave, even when families were broken up. Occasionally, members of the Israeli diplomatic corps were accused of "spying" or "subversion" —charges familiar enough to foreign embassies in Communist capitals—which often turned out to be nothing more than assisting people who were seeking to communicate with relatives or friends in Israel.

In the conflict between Israel and the Arab states, the Soviet Union has continued to give increasing diplomatic and military support to the Arab rulers. Although billions of dollars' worth of arms were lost in the 1967 debacle, Egypt and Syria are being re-equipped with Soviet weapons.

Despite their other differences, both the Soviet Union and the United States initially condemned the Arab aggression in 1948. But they were aligned in the UN against Israel at the time of the Sinai campaign in October, 1956. On the other hand, armed forces of Great Britain and France supported the Sinai drive.

In 1967, the line-up was changed. By backing the Arabs, the Soviets hoped to strengthen their influence in the Near East region. The United States—despite a considerable financial interest in the oil-rich Arab kingdoms—essentially supported Israel. Both great powers, however, asserted Israel's right to exist in spite of the reiterated Arab determination to eliminate the Jewish state.

Great Britain still was disposed to favor Israel in 1967, but France under President de Gaulle lined up with the Arab-Soviet bloc even while the Israeli armies were defeating the Arabs with war planes previously supplied by France.

As the region in which American and Soviet interests converge, in which Britain and France still seek to retain some of their influence, and in which the Arab states are involved in disputes among themselves as well as in internal crises, the Near East remains—to use that cliché of editorialists—a powder keg. Amid the turmoil, the people of Israel have striven to build a stable, prosperous nation. American observers have often suggested that if the great powers would stop sending arms to any nation in the area and insist on peaceful settlement of outstanding differences, the development of the entire region could benefit all the peoples involved.

The antagonism of the Arab states toward Israel is often difficult for Americans to understand. The Arab countries, all members of the United Nations, have never recognized the legal existence of the state of Israel. They have considered themselves at war
with what they term the "occupiers of Palestine"—although the
Palestine partition and Israeli independence were recommended
and voted by the UN General Assembly back in 1947.

In fact, on the very day Israel became a nation, Arab forces
streamed across the borders to kill off the new state in its infancy.
UN Secretary-General Trygve Lie branded the invasion as "aggression" while Arab spokesmen openly boasted that "we have
never concealed the fact that we began the fighting."

After seven months of war, Israel repelled the invaders and
armistice agreements were signed, establishing the boundaries of
the country for the next twenty years. But the conflict brought
internal problems to the warring nations; nearly a million Arabs
left Israel to lead a wretched existence just across the Jordanian
border. Housed in squalid resettlement camps and dependent upon
foreign aid for subsistence, they were armed and encouraged to seek
"revenge" against Israel. They remained a problem to the Arab
rulers, a charge on the international community, and a threat to
Israeli frontier settlements.

More than half a million Jews from the Arab states were com-
pelled to flee their native lands, leaving all their property behind.
Absorbing them in a brief period of time strained the Israeli economy—already seriously burdened by the costs of war—to the break-
ing point.

The armistice agreements, according to their preambles, were
designed to be "the transition to permanent peace." But the Arab
states persisted, as President Nasser of Egypt said in November,

**The Mandelbaum Gate which separated
Israel from Jordan until August, 1967**

1965, to have as their objective the "extermination of Israel." In
the same memorable speech, Nasser threatened the United States
and other nations friendly toward Israel: "The plan to exterminate
Israel is not directed against Israel alone but against those, also,
who stand behind Israel." The Arab states boycotted American
companies trading with Israel and even forbade the showing of
American films featuring performers suspected of pro-Israel sym-
pathies. The Arab rulers falsely told their people that the United
States and Britain fought in support of Israel in 1967.

After the Sinai campaign of 1956, Israel withdrew her forces

behind the borders established by the armistice agreements. A UN
Emergency Force patrolled the Egyptian boundary until 1967,
when the international brigade was withdrawn in response to a
demand by President Nasser. But the frontiers with Syria and
Jordan continued to be the scenes of violent conflict throughout
the years.

At last, fully armed and emboldened, Egypt—according to a
report given in July, 1967 by UN Secretary-General U Thant—
moved toward a renewal of open hostilities. But defeat left the
Arab states even more embittered and unwilling to work out an
overall peace settlement with Israel. The refugee problem was
aggravated and the permanent boundaries of the various nations
in the region are as yet undetermined. But the power relationships
in the Near East were profoundly altered, in ways still not entirely
clear, by the Israeli military and diplomatic victories.

Americans might well wonder what the Arabs have to gain by
prolonging this state of war against Israel. The tangled politics of
the region—the dynastic rivalries, oil concessions, and quarrels over
water rights—can hardly be unraveled in a brief review. But a
major factor is the fear of the absolutist Arab rulers that their own
people will one day want democratic governments similar to
Israel's; that their impoverished subjects will soon demand a
standard of living comparable to that enjoyed by Israel's own pre-
war Arab population of two hundred thousand. Rather than risk
surrendering some of their luxuries and dictatorial powers, the
desert despots prefer to turn the resentments of their people against
a neighboring country and distract their restive populations with
military adventures.

As for Israel, she has offered the Arab states a non-aggression pact, regional disarmament with mutual inspection and control, and technical assistance pending a permanent comprehensive peace settlement. Despite the frequent border "incidents" which killed hundreds of civilians in the years between 1948 and 1967, the period of compulsory military service was shortened and security restrictions in border communities were relaxed, until full-scale war forced Israel to reevaluate its security position. Although surrounded by avowed and outspoken enemies, Israel has refused to adopt a "garrison state" mentality.

Israel's relations with Germany are, to many Israelis, a painful subject for discussion. West Germany paid "reparations" to Israel to compensate for the destruction of Jewish property and lives in World War II. There is active trade between the countries; over fifty thousand German tourists a year visit Israel. Full diplomatic relations were established in 1965, and ambassadors were exchanged.

On the other hand, Israel has demanded that German scientists be restrained from helping Egypt develop weapons of mass destruction and has asked for the continued prosecution of Nazi war criminals. The trial of Adolf Eichmann in 1961 served as an additional reminder of the dreadful events of a generation ago and probably made the normalization of Israeli–German relations more difficult. When the German ambassador—unfortunately a former Nazi officer—arrived at his post, there were popular demonstrations against him.

But Israel's influence on the international scene is most pronounced among the dark-skinned peoples of Africa and Asia. A vigorous opponent of all forms of racial discrimination, Israel has extended economic and technical assistance on the basis of equality

Members of study mission from Guinea receive instruction in fruit cultivation

and mutual respect. Among the projects jointly undertaken have been land reclamation, industrialization, and development of transportation systems. As a small, young nation that "made it," Israel can freely offer help which might be resented if it came from one of the larger powers with a background of imperialism.

Nearly ten thousand trainees from about a hundred countries have been sent to Israel for advanced study. Thousands of Israeli experts have gone abroad. An international conference on the "role of science in the advancement of new states" was convened at the Weizmann Institute in August, 1960; a conference on "comprehensive planning of agriculture in developing countries" was held three years later, while fiscal and monetary policies for the emergent nations was the topic of the Third Rehovot Conference in August, 1965. Presidents, premiers, and cabinet ministers from Asia, Africa, and Latin America are frequent visitors to Israel. And such high-ranking Israeli officials as the prime minister, president, and foreign minister have recently toured Burma, the Congo, Liberia, and other underdeveloped areas.

In aiding these new nations—which in their aggregate contain a fair share of the world's population—Israel has assumed a role in international relations with vast implications for the future. More important, she has kept faith with the traditional teachings of human brotherhood.

Appendix

A BRIEF CHRONOLOGY OF ISRAEL'S HISTORY

ROMAN OCCUPATION *(continued)*   **A.D.**

Crucifixion of Jesus	28
Revolt of the Jews	66-70
Fall of Jerusalem	70
Fall of Masada	73
Revolt of Bar Kochba	132-135
Mishnah completed	200
Rome adopts Christianity; Mohammedanism develops	300-636
Persian Invasion	614-629
Arab Period	636-1099
Crusades	1099-1290
Jews expelled from Spain	1492
Turkish Rule	1516-1918
World War I	1914-1918

ZIONIST MOVEMENT

First Jewish agricultural colony—Petach Tikva	1878
Involvement of Baron de Rothschild	1882
Founding of World Zionist Organization	1897
Tel Aviv (Hill of Spring) founded	1909
First kibbutz established (Degania)	1909
Balfour Declaration	1917
Hebrew University inaugurated	1925
Arab Revolt	1936-1939
Peel Commission Report	1937

British White Paper........................... 1939

Outbreak of World War II..................... 1939

Anglo-American Committee of Inquiry........... 1946

United Nations Partition Resolution.............. 1947

Proclamation of Israel's Independence............ 1948

War of Liberation............................ 1948-1949

Admission to United Nations................... 1949

Election of First Knesset....................... 1949

Chaim Weizmann elected President............. 1949

Armistice Agreements 1949

Adolf Eichmann executed...................... 1962

Pope Paul VI visits Israel...................... 1964

Diplomatic Relations with West Germany......... 1965

President Zalman Shazar visits United States....... 1966

Reprisal Raids on Jordan...................... 1966

David Ben-Gurion visits United States............ 1967

Six-day Israeli-Arab War 1967

Index and Pronunciation Guide